Tips: Organizing, Time Management, Etiquette,
Spirituality, Laughter, Charity & Miscellaneous Tips

ORGANIZING
TIPS
FOR
365 DAYS

With Homework

DEBORAH R. TEBBE

WESTBOW
PRESS®
A DIVISION OF THOMAS NELSON
& ZONDERVAN

WestBow Press books may be ordered through booksellers or by contacting:

WestBow Press
A Division of Thomas Nelson & Zondervan
1663 Liberty Drive
Bloomington, IN 47403
www.westbowpress.com
844-714-3454

To contact author:
www.organizedhappyhelper.com
organizedhh@gmail.com

ISBN: 978-1-6642-8212-4 (sc)
ISBN: 978-1-6642-8213-1 (hc)
ISBN: 978-1-6642-8211-7 (e)

Library of Congress Control Number: 2022919696

Print information available on the last page.

WestBow Press rev. date: 3/15/2023

Dedication

I created this organizing tip calendar as a gift from my Lord Jesus Christ as a way of thanking Him for giving me the inspiration to write it. He planted the vision in me in 2008, and it has taken all these years to see it get published. Better late than never!

Another big inspiration and true friend of mine is Dr. Janet Blakely, Ph.D., an editor of Christian books.

I would also like to thank my husband, John Tebbe, and my family for their support. In addition to encouraging me, they gave me plenty of time to develop my tips. I compiled these recommendations after working with family, friends, and clients over the years. It has been a pleasure guiding my clients and gaining insight into their experiences to provide advice and professional organizing.

Contents

Preface

You may wonder how this book came into existence. I attended a NAPO conference in 2008 where they taught many classes on how to be the best professional organizer.

I noticed a sign in a conference room that said, "Publish a book." I felt inspired and thought about the many avenues and possibilities for this profession. It occurred to me that perhaps I could write a book and publish it one day.

As I thought and prayed on this subject, the Lord Jesus gave me the arrangement in a table with four columns: Date, Category of Tips, and Homework. I needed to compile 365 days of tips gained from working experiences with clients, research from magazines, books, and everyday living.

What's in it for you? Every day you read a tip for that date, apply the homework, and mark it under "Accomplishment: Tip applied and / or Tip mastered with a date. At least try and see if this is something you should keep doing, then work on it until you master it.

Over the course of my career as a Professional Organizer since 2004, I encountered numerous examples of clutter. It's easy to become organized and achieve great results if you are a little unorganized and unhappy with clutter by following these recommendations in **"ORGANIZING TIPS for 365 DAYS, WITH HOMEWORK."** Everyone should have this 365-day calendar on their desk or kitchen counter—especially the chronically disorganized person who wants to learn how to become organized. I have found nothing like my calendar on the market. I teach and train my clients how to organize using a homework method and bin theory.

Every day has a different tip with advice to help you achieve goals that are quick and easy to implement. Homework is explained so that you can DIY and learn how to maintain great work.

If you can accomplish at least twelve tips in this book, you will see how much difference it can make! Master an additional twelve tips under your belt next year. Keep adding these tips every year—that is the purpose of this book—to help you become better organized.

The goal to making a difference in your life is to achieve as many tips as possible so that you have a better organized home, family, and business. You can do it because everyone can be trained. I pray you become the best you can be.

Organization will overflow into other areas in your life.

"His master said to him, 'Well done, good and faithful servant. You have been faithful with a little; I will set you over much. Enter into the joy of your master'" (Matthew 25:21 ESV).

Acknowledgment

I met Dr. Janet Blakely, Ph.D., at church in 1988. We were in the Singles Ministry and became friends. She became a full-time missionary in Europe for eleven years and I supported her in mission-giving during that time. It has come full circle that now she is supporting me as I help to organize her current home. We decided to barter our skills, mine in organizing and hers in editing, so this project could become a reality.

She encouraged me when I was not progressing as fast as I hoped. We edited so many times I can't count. She wanted it well done. I would say, "I don't know if this is worth it," and she would tell me, "This is really going to help people."

Introduction

Debbie Tebbe developed a love for organizing as a little girl. Organizing can be taught with hands-on training using specific explanations and illustrations. It's hard breaking old habits, but it's worth it to make changes to improve your life and apply skills like time management, for example, which we need these days!

Debbie resides in St. Clair Shores, Michigan, (Metropolitan Detroit), with her husband. She has been blessed with three children and four grandchildren. She is a veteran member of the National Association of Productivity & Organizing Professionals (NAPO). It's an organizing company for Professional Organizers to improve their training, education, networking, and attend conferences.

Debbie founded Organizing Happy Helper, LLC to help homeowners and business professionals achieve a clutter-free environment, with peace and joy as a by-product in accomplishing tasks. She became an entrepreneur in 2006 while helping clients navigate the changes in their lives.

Debbie has earned the following certificates from NAPO: Household Management, Residential Organizing, Life Transitions, and ICD: Institute for Challenging Disorganization: Chronically Disorganized Specialist-Level II.

She also is a born-again Christian and has been involved in many ministries including: Chaplain; two years Bible Education in a Discipleship Institute, she ministered in eight mission fields around the world, and many other ministries as a Bible study teacher, a team member of Spiritual Housecleaning, and many more to count.

She is grateful to see this book published, even though it took many years. She gives credit to the Lord, who helped her press on and gave her the strength to endure.

Chapter 1

January

"'For I know the plans that I have for you,' declares the LORD, 'plans for prosperity and not for disaster, to give you a future and a hope'" (Jeremiah 29:11, NASB).

January 1

Time Management

How long does it take to make up a queen-size bed with throw pillows? (This does not include putting on clean sheets.)

Homework

It takes two minutes to make the bed—so make your bed every day, and it will make your room look neater! Get in the habit.

Assignment:

Tip Applied:_____Date: _____
Tip Mastered: _____Date: _____

January 2

Time Management

A Harvard Business Study found that 3% of the class had both written goals and concrete plans. Three percent of the class that had both written goals and a plan were making ten times as much as the rest of the ninety-seven percent of the class.

Homework

Ten years later, thirteen percent of the class that had set written goals but had not created plans, were making twice as much money as the eighty-four percent of the class that had set no goals at all. Write down realistic goals and stick to them. It can work for you too.

Source:
https://www.wanderlustworker.com/the-harvard-mba-business-school-study-on-goal-setting/

Assignment:

Tip Applied:_____Date: _____
Tip Mastered: _____Date: _____

January 3

Organization

It's time to take down the tree and put your Christmas decorations away.

Homework

Take the ornaments off the tree and categorize similar items on a table. Place them in boxes. Take inventory of the ornaments and decorations you don't want anymore, then donate them, or give them to someone starting out.

Assignment:

Tip Applied:_____Date: _____
Tip Mastered: _____Date: _____

January 4

Tip

Every day, use a clean dishcloth and dish towel to wipe down dishes, counters, and tables to prevent germs.

Homework

Stay on top of your laundry so that you have clean dish towels and dishcloths on hand when needed.

Assignment:

Tip Applied:_____Date: _____
Tip Mastered: _____Date: _____

January 5

Organization

In hot water, separate your dark-colored towels from your light-colored ones to prevent bleeding.

Homework

The best results can be achieved by sorting your laundry. It is not a good idea to wash towels with sweaters, delicate fabric garments, and so forth. Fuzzy balls will appear on the clothing.

Assignment:

Tip Applied:_____Date: _____
Tip Mastered: _____Date: _____

January 6

Spirituality

Pray before every meal, thanking God for the food you eat. By doing so, you will ensure that your food is blessed and safe from harm.

"Do not be anxious about anything, but in everything by prayer and supplication with thanksgiving let your requests be made known to God" (Philippians 4:6, ESV).

Homework

Even if you pray silently to yourself, pray every day and three times a day at every meal.

Assignment:

Tip Applied:_____Date: _____
Tip Mastered: _____Date: _____

January 7

Organization

Take a few moments before you leave for work or begin your day to make your bed, put away toiletries, and put clothes in the hamper / laundry basket to tidy up.

Homework

These small chores take only fifteen minutes per day to complete. When you are finished, your house will be neat and tidy, and you will start a successful habit. There is nothing better than coming home to an organized house.

Assignment:

Tip Applied:_____Date: _____
Tip Mastered: _____Date: _____

January 8

Tip

Make sure you get your annual checkup every year (e.g., an annual physical exam, plus a mammogram and pap test for women).

Homework

Many people schedule their doctor appointments during their birthday week to remind themselves.

Assignment:

Tip Applied:_____Date: _____
Tip Mastered: _____Date: _____

January 9

Time Management

Once you've completed painting for the day, wrap your rollers, brushes, and painting tools in plastic wrap so they can be used the next day. This will allow you to begin painting without washing the tools again. You can continue painting where you left off.

Homework

Please don't procrastinate if you don't want your rollers and brushes to become stiff!

Assignment:

Tip Applied:_____Date: _____
Tip Mastered: _____Date: _____

January 10

Time Management

Does your family need a calendar? There are applications and wall calendars to choose from. Time will come when you need to teach your children the value of responsibility.

Homework

The color-coding feature helps you keep track of each member's appointments, assignments, and tasks through the respective colors assigned to them. Plus, you can share your menu plans, chores, and to-do lists. You can coordinate and edit simultaneously so that nothing is missed!

Assignment:

Tip Applied:_____Date: _____
Tip Mastered: _____Date: _____

January 11

Spirituality

In your Bible, you might consider writing notes along with a highlighter.

"This is what the Lord, the God of Israel says: 'Write all the words which I have spoken to you in a book'" (Jeremiah 30:2, NASB).

Homework

If you attend a church service, Bible study, retreats, or seminars, write the date and location next to the Scripture. It will bring back memories each time you reread it.

Assignment:

Tip Applied:_____Date: _____

Tip Mastered: _____Date: _____

Laughter

My husband and I were in the vehicle with my ten-year-old granddaughter in the back seat. I said to him, "If we do it this way, we can kill two birds with one stone." My granddaughter spoke up and wept, "Grandma, why would you ever want to kill a bird?"

Source:
Debbie Tebbe

Q. Why did the unemployed man get excited about reading his Bible?
A. He thought he saw a Job.

Q. Who was the greatest babysitter mentioned in the Bible?
A. David, he rocked Goliath to a very deep sleep.

Source:
https://christiancamppro.com/the-constantly-growing-list-of-funny-christian-jokes-with-pictures/

January 13

Time Management

Make sure your bank deposits are ready in the office or at home for cashing or depositing checks. Pick up extra forms at the bank so you have them on hand.

Homework

The drive-through or the bank will save you time. Debit cards are now being used instead of deposit slips by some banks and / or ATMs.

Assignment:

Tip Applied:_____Date: _____
Tip Mastered: _____Date: _____

January 14

Organization

Everything and anything can be stored in plastic bins of all sizes. It protects its contents from floods, water sewage, tornadoes, hurricanes, and bugs. Label each clear bin to know exactly what is inside.

Homework

Plastic bins with see-through lids can be purchased, filled, labelled, and stacked for storage. Store them on shelves to prevent water from getting inside. Consider hiring a professional organizer if necessary.

Assignment:

Tip Applied:_____Date: _____
Tip Mastered: _____Date: _____

January 15

Tip

Get your eyes examined at least every two years.

Homework

To maintain a lifetime of healthy vision, adults ages 18 to 60 years old should have a comprehensive eye exam at least once every two years. Older adults (ages 65 and older) should have annual eye exams. "At risk" adults should have an exam at least once every year, or as recommended by their doctor. Plan ahead and budget money for new glasses or contact lenses; schedule your appointment.

Assignment:

Tip Applied:_____Date: _____
Tip Mastered: _____Date: _____

January 16

Time Management

Prepare banana or zucchini bread in pans, let them sit overnight in the refrigerator, and then bake them the following morning. Hot bread will be served for breakfast, and the house will smell homey.

Homework

Plan your time and prepare the bread the night before—this will save you time in the morning. It can be fun to bake a great loaf of bread for friends and family.

Assignment:

Tip Applied:_____Date: _____
Tip Mastered: _____Date: _____

January 17

Tip

Save money and electricity by turning off the lights when leaving a room.

Homework

You should try to turn off the lights when not in use. Invest in LED lights since they are more energy-efficient and save money.

I remember my mom always saying, "Turn off the lights, I'm not married to Edison."

Assignment:

Tip Applied:_____Date: _____
Tip Mastered: _____Date: _____

January 18

Spirituality

Read your Bible every day—a verse, a chapter, or a book. It will be worthwhile as you grow spiritually.

Homework

"All Scripture is breathed out by God and profitable for teaching, for reproof, for correction, and for training in righteousness" (2 Timothy 3:16, ESV).

Assignment:

Tip Applied:_____Date: _____

Tip Mastered: _____Date: _____

January 19

Laughter

"The man says, 'I work, and you stay at home, so you should make the coffee.' The woman replies, 'Well, the Bible says men are supposed to make coffee.' 'Really?' asks the man. The woman takes out a Bible and flips to the page, then says, 'See? (He-brews.)'"

Source:
https://christiancamppro.com/the-constantly-growing-list-of-funny-christian-jokes-with-pictures/

January 20

Time Management

Run the lawnmower over your sidewalk when cutting the grass, and the cut grass will be picked up.

Homework

You can also use a blower or a broom to sweep up. For even better results, if you're using a side-shooting mower, direct the discharge away from the driveway. Take the extra step to keep your lawn looking well-maintained and manicured.

Assignment:

Tip Applied:_____Date: _____
Tip Mastered: _____Date: _____

January 21

Tip

Take the time to work hard each day and see what you can accomplish this week. Be amazed at your abilities and talents and see what you can achieve.

Homework

Establish goals for small, everyday things and accomplish as many as you can.

Assignment:

Tip Applied:_____Date: _____
Tip Mastered: _____Date: _____

January 22

Organization

Glass, plastic containers, and newspapers should all be recycled. When disposing of trash, separate it. In the kitchen you should have two trash cans (one recycling can, and one trash can).

Homework

Our mission is to save the Earth one person and one item at a time. The earth urges you to recycle!

Assignment:

Tip Applied:_____Date: _____
Tip Mastered: _____Date: _____

January 23

Time Management

Wash dirty clothes by color: socks, underwear, T-shirts, and sheets, should all be washed in hot water to kill dust mites and soiled stains.

Homework

When you wash a full load, you'll save on water, electricity, and gas for the dryer.

Assignment:

Tip Applied:_____Date: _____
Tip Mastered: _____Date: _____

January 24

Organization

After every meal, each family member should rinse their dishes in the sink, throw away bones, rinds, napkins, and anything else that does not go down the garbage disposal. Load the dishes in the dishwasher.

Homework

Have a family meeting to organize the daily chores and work together as a team.

Assignment:

Tip Applied:_____Date: _____
Tip Mastered: _____Date: _____

January 25

Tip

Maintain a budget to pay your bills on time. Overspending your income will cause you to fall behind on your bills.

Homework

Five steps to creating a budget:

- List your income
- List your expenses
- Subtract expenses from income
- Tract your expenses (all month long)
- Make a new budget before the month begins

Dave Ramsey is a great source and very financially detailed.

Source:
https://www.ramseysolutions.com/budgeting/guide-to-budgeting/how-to-create-a-budget

Assignment:

Tip Applied:_____Date: _____
Tip Mastered: _____Date: _____

January 26

Organization

The dishwasher helps prevent the spread of colds and viruses by sanitizing dishes.

Homework

Running the dishwasher when full will help you conserve water, soap, and electricity. Be sure to load the dishwasher every day. Now who is going to unload the dishwasher and put the dishes away?

Assignment:

Tip Applied:_____Date: _____
Tip Mastered: _____Date: _____

January 27

Laughter

People can sing or whistle anywhere and everywhere you go—in your vehicle, at home, at work, or just for fun. Women frequently whistle while cleaning, cooking, and getting ready for the day.

Homework

It creates contentment and happiness to be around people who whistle and sing. Try it—you'll make someone else happy as well.

Assignment:

Tip Applied:_____Date: _____
Tip Mastered: _____Date: _____

January 28

Spirituality

Placing a Bible under your pillow will give you God's peace if you have nightmares, bad dreams, or are afraid to go to sleep.

"The LORD is my light and my salvation; whom shall, I fear? The LORD is the stronghold of my life; of whom shall I be afraid?" (Psalm 27:1, ESV).

Homework

Also, you can add a cross—though some people laugh at this—but it has spiritual significance, and it works! I encourage you to give it a try!

Assignment:

Tip Applied:_____Date: _____
Tip Mastered: _____Date: _____

January 29

Etiquette

Keep your hands clean by washing them with soap and water. Hands are a source of many germs that can cause infections. Handwashing can prevent about thirty percent of diarrhea-related illnesses and about twenty percent of respiratory infections (e.g., colds).

Homework

Here are some strong suggestions for when to wash your hands:

- Before, during, and after preparing and eating food
- Before and after caring for someone at home who is sick with vomiting or diarrhea and treating a cut or wound
- After using the toilet, changing diapers, or cleaning up a child who has used the toilet
- When blowing your nose, coughing, or sneezing
- Coming in contact with animals, animal waste, or animal feed, and handling pet food or treats
- After touching garbage
- Use hand sanitizer when you can't wash your hands

Implement this rule in your daily life if you haven't already. It's essential that we follow proper washing and sanitizing methods especially when it comes to the Coronavirus.

Source:
https://www.cdc.gov/handwashing/when-how-handwashing.html

Assignment:

Tip Applied:_____Date: _____
Tip Mastered: _____Date: _____

January 30

Tip

To keep your hair healthy and looking great, salon stylists recommend getting your hair cut or trimmed every four to six weeks for short hair and every six to eight weeks for longer hair.

Homework

During checkout, ask the cashier to schedule your next hair appointment. Write it down on your calendar to avoid forgetting it.

Assignment:

Tip Applied:_____Date: _____
Tip Mastered: _____Date: _____

January 31

Charity & Spirituality

Charity definition:

"Generosity and helpfulness, especially toward the needy or suffering; aid given to those in need; an institution engaged in relief for the poor."

Homework

Millions of people around the world are hungry, poor, and do not have enough food to get them through the next day. We should consider how blessed we are by being able to help others. Some people in our country are suffering from the loss of their jobs and need your help. You can do this by contributing to a food pantry, financial giving, and volunteering to spread love.

Assignment:

Tip Applied:_____Date: _____
Tip Mastered: _____Date: _____

Chapter 2

February

Finally, be strong in the Lord and in the strength of His might. Put on the full armor of God, so that you will be able to stand firm against the schemes of the devil. For our struggle is not against flesh and blood, but against the rulers, against the powers, against the world forces of this darkness, against the spiritual forces of wickedness in the heavenly places. Therefore, take up the full armor of God, so that you will be able to resist on the evil day, and having done everything, to stand firm. Stand firm therefore, having belted your waist with truth, and having put on the breastplate of righteousness, and having strapped on your feet the preparation of the gospel of peace; in addition to all, taking up the shield of faith with which you will be able to extinguish all the flaming arrows of the evil one. And take the helmet of salvation and the sword of the Spirit, which is the word of God. (Ephesians 6:10-17 NASB)

February 1

Organization

Did you know stuffed closets are bad for your health? It is hard to breathe or make air circulate due to the clutter.

According to research, four psychological effects of clutter are:

- Stress and increased cortisol levels can become long-term
- Feelings of shame or inadequacy that can lead to depression
- Distraction from focus kills our productivity
- Negative behavioral effects for ourselves and our children

Homework

Corresponding to these psychological effects, each time you look around and feel anxious that the mess is getting out of control, your body releases cortisol, one of the classic stress hormones.

The clutter could also be contributing to conditions like asthma. Start now to declutter your closet.

Source:
https://miadanielle.com/psychological-effects-of-clutter/

Assignment:

Tip Applied:_____Date: _____
Tip Mastered: _____Date: _____

February 2

Organization

Place horizontal wire racks in the kitchen cupboard to hold dishes, mugs, bowls, and glasses. They will be less likely to chip or break.

Homework

It will be easier to stack them and you'll have more space.

Assignment:

Tip Applied:_____Date: _____
Tip Mastered: _____Date: _____

February 3

Etiquette

If someone is kind to you or performs a large favor, let them know how grateful you are.

Homework

Show your appreciation by sending a thank-you note and / or card within a week.

Assignment:

Tip Applied:_____Date: _____
Tip Mastered: _____Date: _____

February 4

Charity & Spirituality

Make a donation of clothes and household items.

"Give, and it will be given to you. They will pour into your lap a good measure—pressed down, shaken together and running over. For by your standard of measure it will be measured to you in return" (Luke 6:38, NASB).

Homework

Take time to consider those in need. Someone else's junk is someone else's treasure. You can donate a lot of good items that you no longer use. No one can outdo God! Make the most of your Good Samaritan nature by helping others as much as possible. Giving is also mentioned in this verse. The Lord loves cheerful givers! The storehouse belongs to Him, and He will always provide for you.

Assignment:

Tip Applied:_____Date: _____
Tip Mastered: _____Date: _____

February 5

Tip

Every two weeks, gently massage a deep conditioner into your hair. Let it sit for ten minutes. As a result, your hair will shine, feel soft, and have damaged ends repaired.

Homework

You don't have to have brittle hair. Just pamper yourself.

Assignment:

Tip Applied:_____Date: _____
Tip Mastered: _____Date: _____

 # February 6

Laughter

Q. Who was the best businesswoman in the Bible?
A. Pharaoh's daughter. She went down to the Bank of the Nile and drew out a little prophet.

Q. What do they call Pastors in Germany?
A. German Shepherds

Q. Why didn't they play cards on the ark?
A. Because Noah was always standing on the deck.

Source:
https://christiancamppro.com/the-constantly-growing-list-of-funny-christian-jokes-with-pictures/

February 7

Organization

In your vehicle glove compartment, place loose items in a tray.

Homework

Vehicle organizers can be purchased online. Organize your car by placing items in the tray. Don't forget the litter bag. Always keep your updated registration and insurance card in case you need it.

Assignment:

Tip Applied:_____Date: _____
Tip Mastered: _____Date: _____

February 8

Spirituality

"Count it all joy, my brothers, when you meet trials of various kinds, for you know that the testing of your faith produces steadfastness." And let steadfastness have its full effect, that you may be perfect and complete, lacking in nothing" (James 1:2-4, ESV).

Homework

Who has pure joy while going through a trial?

Often, we need to change our attitude from one of negativity to that of positivity. Perhaps the Lord is testing us or something better is ahead.

Assignment:

Tip Applied:_____Date: _____
Tip Mastered: _____Date: _____

February 9

Tip

Are you getting too many telemarketing calls on your mobile and landline phone?

Homework

Contact the "National Do Not Call Registry" at <u>www.donotcall.gov</u>. Fill out the easy form. It takes thirty-one days to become active.

Assignment:

Tip Applied:_____Date: _____
Tip Mastered: _____Date: _____

February 10

Tip

Are you being scammed?

- Imposter Scams
- Tech Support Scams
- Grandkid Scams
- IRS Imposter Scams
- Online Dating Scams
- Email Scams
- Coronavirus Scams

Homework

Please report scams and frauds if you spot one. Alert the Federal Trade Commission. Report a scam online or call the FTC at 1-877-FTC-HELP.

If you receive an email from your credit card company that you made a large charge, their phone number takes you straight to the scammer. They are so professional and compassionate that you don't know the difference. Check your account first before making any calls to them.

Also, if you won a prize, the return email address has nothing to do with your accounts. Send to scam and unsubscribe. Don't open it because they have a way of knowing this to trick you.

Source:
https://reportfraud.ftc.gov/#/

Assignment:

Tip Applied:_____Date: _____
Tip Mastered: _____Date: _____

February 11

Organization

What do you do with yellow and white telephone directories delivered to your door?

Homework

Remove the old versions and replace them with new ones. The old phonebooks can be recycled. Do not pile up years of yellow pages; they take up valuable space.

Assignment:

Tip Applied:_____Date: _____
Tip Mastered: _____Date: _____

February 12

Etiquette

What is a reasonable tip for a restaurant?

Homework

- Ten percent if you liked the meal but thought the service was inadequate
- Fifteen percent if you were pleased with the meal and the service was fast
- Twenty percent if the food was exceptional and the service was impeccable
- If terrible service, call the manager over and most likely they will take care of the bill or offer a free dessert
- If fantastic service, call the manager over and brag on the server

Assignment:

Tip Applied:_____Date: _____

Tip Mastered: _____Date: _____

February 13

Tip

Cleaning the office every Friday before you go home and / or your home office is a good habit.

Homework

Cleaning your desk, cabinets, file drawers, and computer with disinfecting wipes is essential. Do not forget to wash your coffee mug. After you leave the office, it will be sparkling clean.

Assignment:

Tip Applied:_____Date: _____
Tip Mastered: _____Date: _____

February 14

Charity

Today is Valentine's Day.

Purchase flowers, candy, balloons, and a card for someone today.

Homework

Is there no one in your life to share Valentine's Day with? Purchase something for your children, parents, or a friend to make them happy. The joy they experience will make you feel better.

Assignment:

Tip Applied:_____Date: _____
Tip Mastered: _____Date: _____

February 15

Etiquette

Following through on your promises when volunteering means staying on schedule.

Homework

Be careful not to sign up for a project, ministry, or anything else that won't fit into your schedule or that you can't handle. Please pray first before committing to something. If you fail to complete your job, another person will have to take over.

Assignment:

Tip Applied:_____Date: _____
Tip Mastered: _____Date: _____

February 16

Charity

"For you formed my inward parts; you knitted me together in my mother's womb. I praise you, for I am fearfully and wonderfully made. Wonderful are your works; my soul knows it very well. My frame was not hidden from you, when I was being made in secret, intricately woven in the depths of the earth. Your eyes saw my unformed substance; in your book were written, every one of them, the days that were formed for me, when as yet there was none of them" (Psalm 139:13-16, ESV).

Homework

Every baby is knitted and formed in its mother's womb. No matter what, everyone is special, even if they've suffered a miscarriage or a loss. They will be taken directly to heaven to rest in Jesus' arms.

This is what Jesus told me was a great idea for a pro-life vehicle sticker against abortion:

"A baby today in a mother's womb, has now become a baby's tomb."

Visit a crisis pregnancy center in your area for help with counseling, ultrasounds, layettes, volunteering, and donations.

Assignment:

Tip Applied:_____Date: _____
Tip Mastered: _____Date: _____

February 17

Laugher

Smile at people as they pass you by, look directly at them and smile—see how many smiles you receive in return. There's a possibility that the only smile they received all day was yours. Perhaps your kindness brightened their day.

Homework

Make eye contact with everyone and smile at them. It will make you and them feel happy and blessed.

Assignment:

Tip Applied:_____Date: _____
Tip Mastered: _____Date: _____

February 18

Tip

Are you suffering from anxiety? The key is to keep busy. Getting things done helps people forget about their problems and helps them focus on what's important.

Homework

Break the cycle of worry:

- Get moving by exercising
- Take a yoga or tai chi class
- Meditate and pray
- Apply progressive muscle relaxation
- Practice deep breathing
- Talk to a trustworthy person about your worries

"The upset person must escape himself in battle, or he weakens with no hope."

Source:
www.helpguide.org/articles/anxiety/how-to-stop-worrying.htm

Assignment:

Tip Applied:_____Date: _____
Tip Mastered: _____Date: _____

February 19

Organization

How do I choose the right hangers to use? When you hang your clothes on a hanger, do they fall off? When you wear them, do they make angel wings on your shoulders?

Homework

Consider thin velvet types, Joy Hangers, and / or for men big plastic hangers you see on the racks of clothes at the stores. Your clothes will stay on hangers, and you will save space in the closet. The hangers are affordable and functional.

Assignment:

Tip Applied:_____Date: _____
Tip Mastered: _____Date: _____

February 20

Tip

Purchase Super Sliders to move furniture which rolls on carpet, hardwood floors, tile, and laminate.

Homework

When you need to move heavy furniture, just place the sliders under the legs and push. Save your carpet and rug surfaces from snags and tears. They glide effortlessly across carpeted surfaces. You don't have to be strong to push across the floor.

Assignment:

Tip Applied:_____Date: _____
Tip Mastered: _____Date: _____

February 21

Spirituality

Where does the 80/20 rule apply at your church?

"Even as the Son of Man came not to be served but to serve, and to give his life as a ransom for many" (Matthew 20:28, ESV).

Homework

A common saying in the Christian community is that twenty percent of the people do eighty percent of the work. The issue of burnout arises when you are always pulling from the same group of people. Get involved and volunteer!

Assignment:

Tip Applied:_____Date: _____
Tip Mastered: _____Date: _____

February 22

Laughter

Have you ever seen someone leave a restroom with toilet paper stuck to the bottom of his or her shoe, dangling off their pants? That is hilarious, and I have to laugh. Once I have gathered my composure, I usually tell them.

- What if Jesus was Irish: 1. He never got married. 2. He never held a steady job. 3. His last request was for a drink.
- What if Jesus was Italian: 1. He talked with his hands. 2. He had wine at every meal. 3. He worked in the garden.
- What if Jesus was Californian: 1. He never cuts his hair. 2. He walked around barefoot. 3. He invented a new religion.
- Jesus was Jewish: 1. He went into his father's business. 2. He lived at home until the age of 33. 3. He was sure his mother was a virgin, and his mother was sure that he was God.

Source:
https://www.javacasa.com/humor/miscell.htm

February 23

Tip

If you have a worry problem, apply the following formula.

Homework

1. Ask yourself, "What is the worst that can possibly happen?"
2. Prepare to accept the worst if it is necessary.
3. Peaceably proceed to improve the outcome.
4. Above all, pray that the Lord will take it in the palms of his hands and carry it for you.
5. Most of the time, the worst never happens.

Assignment:

Tip Applied:_____Date: _____
Tip Mastered: _____Date: _____

February 24

Tip

On a hot day, never leave your child or pet in a vehicle. They could die from the heat.

Homework

Before exiting, check the vehicle for children or pets. Try to imagine yourself sitting inside a hot vehicle. There are often reports in the news about children and pets still being abused like this. Such people could face jail and may cause the death of loved ones!

Assignment:

Tip Applied:_____Date: _____
Tip Mastered: _____Date: _____

February 25

Tip

Have you noticed moths eating your wool jackets or other clothing?

Homework

In your closet, put lavender seeds and / or moth balls in a sachet.

Assignment:

Tip Applied:_____Date: _____
Tip Mastered: _____Date: _____

February 26

Spirituality

"Behold, I stand at the door and knock. If anyone hears my voice and opens the door, I will come in to him and eat with him, and he with me" (Revelation 3:20, ESV).

Homework

This verse is so important because when you open the door, Jesus wants to have fellowship with you. Accept His invitation—ask Jesus into your heart and submit to His will in your life.

Assignment:

Tip Applied:_____Date: _____
Tip Mastered: _____Date: _____

February 27

Organization

Do you feel ill because of your crammed drawers and closets? Are you unable to close them properly because they are so full?

Homework

You can organize one drawer or a set of drawers in your dresser at a time. If you have more time, continue organizing. Particularly, if you are in the mood.

Assignment:

Tip Applied:_____Date: _____

Tip Mastered: _____Date: _____

February 28

Tip

How green is your home for recycling?

Homework

Each year, Americans throw away nearly thirty percent of their waste as recyclable paper. Glass bottles and / or containers can be recycled again and again. Recycle for the sake of the environment so that your children and grandchildren can enjoy the earth.

Assignment:

Tip Applied:_____Date: _____
Tip Mastered: _____Date: _____

February 29

Organization

The linen closet should be organized.

Homework

Getting rid of ripped sheets and faded or torn towels is a great idea. You can double the amount of storage space by rolling towels to place them on shelves. Sort sheets by bed size and place them into containers or baskets and label them. Additionally, you can donate them to animal humane shelters.

Assignment:

Tip Applied:_____Date: _____
Tip Mastered: _____Date: _____

Chapter 3

March

"Finally, brothers and sisters, whatever is true, whatever is honorable, whatever is right, whatever is pure, whatever is lovely, whatever is commendable, if there is any excellence and if anything worthy of praise, think about these things (Philippians 4:8, NASB).

March 1

Charity

Many clients ask what you do with old prescription eyeglasses. Millions living in low and middle-income countries lack access to basic eye care services. Lions Clubs have recognized the urgent need for corrective lenses and collect usable glasses in their communities to support the Lions Recycle for Sight Program.

Homework

Send your collected eyeglasses to an official Lions Eyeglass Recycling Center (LERC) for processing. There, the glasses are sorted to determine those that are usable or unusable, processed, and placed in inventory for distribution to optical missions around the world. Lions help to minimize landfill waste by supporting precious metal reclamation and scrap processing for damaged glasses that are unusable.

Source:
https://www.lionsclubs.org/en/resources-for-members/resource-center/recycle-eyeglasses

Assignment:

Tip Applied:_____Date: _____
Tip Mastered: _____Date: _____

March 2

Spiritual & Laughter

"A joyful heart is good medicine, but a crushed spirit dries up the bones" (Proverbs 17:22, ESV).

Homework

Studies so far have shown that laughter can help relieve pain, bring greater happiness, and even increase immunity. Try to laugh as much as you can. Watch comedy shows and / or read funny stories.

Assignment:

Tip Applied:_____Date: _____
Tip Mastered: _____Date: _____

March 3

Spirituality

"Jesus said to him, 'I am the way, and the truth, and the life; no one comes to the Father except through Me" (John 14:6, ESV).

Jesus is the only way to the throne of God. He is the only way to get to heaven. There are no other gods before Him. He is the only God that rose from the dead. Other gods are idols and are still in the grave.

March 4

Organization

Most women have fancy purses or designer clutches that they use for weddings, parties, or other gatherings.

Homework

Taking good care of your evening purses will ensure you can pass them on to your children or grandchildren. They never go out of style. Store them in a plastic bin with a lid. They are all accessible in one place whenever you need a purse.

Assignment:

Tip Applied:_____Date: _____
Tip Mastered: _____Date: _____

March 5

Laughter

An organization project I did for a client was organizing a closet. A large, engraved trophy cup stood proudly at the top of the shelf. As I was cleaning the dust from the trophy, I asked the client whose it was. She said, "My Mom's." I asked her how she got it. She replied, "It's her ashes!" I shuddered inside and couldn't wait to put it down and forget about it!

Source:
Debbie Tebbe

I was driving down a highway when suddenly I came upon a church that had a sign out front that read: "Have trouble sleeping? Come hear one of our sermons!"

Source:
https://www.javacasa.com/humor/miscell.htm

March 6

Time Management

Are you recycling junk mail, or do you keep it with your pile of important mail?

Homework

From the mailbox, place the junk mail directly in the recycle bin. Many people keep it with their piles of mail and after a week or two, the pile is overwhelming. They procrastinate to sort it out.

Assignment:

Tip Applied:_____Date: _____

Tip Mastered: _____Date: _____

March 7

Tip

How often should you wash the pillows on your beds?

Homework

Whatever your pillow is filled with, they are repositories for all kinds of fungal spores, perspiration, drool—not to mention dust mites. Most pillows can be thrown in the washing machine in hot water, and then use medium heat in the dryer. They will come out fluffy and smelling fresh. It's recommended you do this twice a year.

Assignment:

Tip Applied:_____Date: _____
Tip Mastered: _____Date: _____

March 8

Organization

Are your cosmetic brushes and makeup taking over your drawers and counter space?

Homework

You can purchase clear, makeup organizers and storage stackable acrylic bins with divided drawers for your makeup. It is so easy and effective. You can find these storage drawers at stores like HomeGoods and Marshalls for the lowest prices.

Assignment:

Tip Applied:_____Date: _____
Tip Mastered: _____Date: _____

March 9

Laughter

Q. Who was the greatest comedian in the Bible?
A. Samson. He brought the house down.

Q. Who was the greatest financier in the Bible?
A. Noah. He was floating his stock while everyone else was in liquidation.

Q. What time of day was Adam created?
A. Just a little before Eve.

Source:
https://christiancamppro.com/the-constantly-growing-list-of-funny-christian-jokes-with-pictures/

March 10

Spirituality

"And the Lord answered me: 'Write the vision; make it plain on tablets, so he may run who reads it'" (Habakkuk 2:2, ESV).

"Where there is no prophetic vision, the people cast off restraint: but blessed is he who keeps the law" (Proverbs 29:18, ESV).

Homework

When you have an idea or dream write it down and / or tear out the picture of it from a magazine or news article.

- A godly vision is right for the times, church, and the people.
- A godly vision promotes faith rather than fear; vision motivates people to action.
- A godly vision requires risk-taking, and glorifies God, not people.
- Create a vision board, write down your idea, and post pictures.

Place your board where you will see it daily. Your dreams will come true.

Assignment:

Tip Applied:_____Date: _____
Tip Mastered: _____Date: _____

March 11

Time Management

Replace or clean the filters for your furnace, vacuums, HVAC system, and air-purifier.

Homework

Write the date of filter replacement some place where you can find it. You can note it on your calendar or the appliance itself.

Assignment:

Tip Applied:_____Date: _____
Tip Mastered: _____Date: _____

March 12

Tip

Do you know how much bacteria are on a kitchen sponge?

Homework

Ten million bacteria per square inch! It's two hundred thousand times dirtier than the toilet seat! To kill the bacteria, microwave on high for one minute every other day or toss it in the dishwasher. Throw it away when it starts to fray or smell.

Source:
https://www.wsj.com/articles/kitchen-sponge-confidential-1386029092

Assignment:

Tip Applied:_____Date: _____
Tip Mastered: _____Date: _____

March 13

Organization & Time Management

Greeting cards are easy to organize by categories, saving you money and time.

Homework

Purchase a greeting card box or oversized shoe box. Use large index card dividers and label each one according to the card category. Place individual cards in their category. When you need a card, select it from the box. This saves a trip to the store and saves money.

Assignment:

Tip Applied:_____Date: _____
Tip Mastered: _____Date: _____

March 14

Tip

Save money and print your own photos.

Homework

Most printers today have color and photo settings. Buy 4x6 inch and letter size photo paper. Your tray will adjust to the size of the paper. Print and distribute or frame photos for your loved ones.

Assignment:

Tip Applied:_____Date: _____
Tip Mastered: _____Date: _____

March 15

Tip

Do you take vitamins or supplements daily?

Homework

There are hundreds of vitamins to choose from—something for each and every ailment. Start taking them and get healthy!

Assignment:

Tip Applied:_____Date: _____
Tip Mastered: _____Date: _____

March 16

Organization

Color-code all your school subjects. For example, for history class, use blue paper tablets, blue report covers and / or binders, blue post-it notes, blue highlighters, and so forth.

Homework

Color-coding school subjects serves as a visual aid. As a result, you will know what subject you need to work on for the class and be able to quickly find the colored school supplies you need. Keep each category together so it is "grab-and-go."

Assignment:

Tip Applied:_____Date: _____

Tip Mastered: _____Date: _____

March 17

Spirituality

"For by grace you have been saved through faith. And this is not your own doing; it is the gift of God, not a result of works, so that no one may boast" (Ephesians 2:8-9, ESV).

Homework

Many people believe that going to heaven is based on being a good person or working our way there. It is actually a free gift from God for those who ask for salvation and eternal life.

Assignment:

Tip Applied:_____Date: _____

Tip Mastered: _____Date: _____

March 18

Laughter

Q. If Mary had Jesus, and Jesus is the Lamb of God,
A. Does that mean Mary had a little lamb?

Q. Why did Noah have to punish and discipline the chickens on the Ark?
A. They were using foul language.

Q. Why didn't Jonah trust the ocean?
A. He just knew there was something fishy about it.

Source:
https://christiancamppro.com/the-constantly-growing-list-of-funny-christian-jokes-with-pictures/

March 19

Tip

Today is Poison Prevention Day. Do you have your medications and cleaning products locked away?

Homework

Use child safety locks for cupboards, drawers, and lock products inside. Keep them high and out of reach with toddlers and small children. You would be surprised how some children still open cupboards with safety devices.

My 18-month-old son used to climb on top of the refrigerator. There is no limit to how far they will go to test you.

Assignment:

Tip Applied:_____Date: _____
Tip Mastered: _____Date: _____

March 20

Organization

Everyone is entitled to have one junk drawer. You can still use a desk organizer to keep it arranged.

Homework

Purchase dividers, boxes, desk organizer trays, or small containers to sort and categorize the items in the junk drawer.

Assignment:

Tip Applied:_____Date: _____

Tip Mastered: _____Date: _____

March 21

Organization

Sort dark-colored jeans, pants, shirts, blouses, and sweatshirts together. Wash sweaters separately.

Homework

Organize your laundry by sorting the categories for permanent press versus items that need to be ironed.

Assignment:

Tip Applied:_____Date: _____
Tip Mastered: _____Date: _____

March 22

Organization & Time Management

Set out all ingredients you'll need before you start baking. After using an ingredient, place it back in the baking container and clean up as you go.

Homework

Store supplies in a baking container separate from cooking spices. It's easy to find when they are categorized. It saves time and makes it easier to clean up messes before they stick to the counter.

Assignment:

Tip Applied:_____Date: _____
Tip Mastered: _____Date: _____

March 23

Charity

Red Cross Giving Day.

March 23rd is the American Red Cross Giving Day, when they recognize the people who make their mission possible—volunteers, blood donors, people trained in lifesaving skills and their supporters—who step up to aid others.

Homework

Take Red Cross certification classes to learn how to save a life in different emergencies. Prepare for the unexpected! They also need your help with blood donations!

Assignment:

Tip Applied:_____Date: _____
Tip Mastered: _____Date: _____

March 24

Spirituality

"Not neglecting to meet together, as is the habit of some, but encouraging one another, and all the more as you see the Day drawing near" (Hebrews 10:25, ESV).

Homework

It's important to keep up your spiritual life by going to church, even though it seems hectic during the week. Go to a later service or mass to be fed spiritually so you can get through the week—otherwise you'll become weak!

Assignment:

Tip Applied:_____Date: _____
Tip Mastered: _____Date: _____

March 25

Laughter

Q. What excuse did Adam give his children about why he no longer lived in Eden?
A. Your mother ate us out of the house and home!

Q. How do groups of angels greet each other?
A. Halo, halo, halo!

Q. How long did Cain hate his brother?
A. As long as he was Able.

Source:
https://christiancamppro.com/the-constantly-growing-list-of-funny-christian-jokes-with-pictures/

March 26

Organization

I have a lot of jewelry. What do I do with it all?

Homework

A nice jewelry box or armoire will help you organize your jewelry. Put earrings by color in the divided box sections. This will make finding earrings to match your outfit easier and quicker. You can do the same with bracelets and necklaces.

Assignment:

Tip Applied:_____Date: _____
Tip Mastered: _____Date: _____

March 27

Organization

Keep all your warranties, manuals, receipts, and serial numbers together for appliances.

Homework

Sort all your warranties in a filing system so you can locate them when needed. You can also organize them by various rooms to find them faster. For example, the kitchen file includes kitchen appliances, set of pans, and table sets. Bedroom file includes mattress, linens, furniture, clock, and so forth.

Assignment:

Tip Applied:_____Date: _____
Tip Mastered: _____Date: _____

March 28

Organization

Did you know that there are unusual items you can clean in the dishwasher?

Homework

For example: Baseball caps, flip-flops, plastic hairbrush and comb, plastic baby toys, toothbrush and holder, garden tool for house plants; also, kitchen tools such as scrub brushes, refrigerator components such as butter tray and small crisper drawers; metal vent covers and some vacuum cleaner attachments (check owner's manual first). Wash on sanitizer setting and you shouldn't have any worries of bacteria.

Source:
https://www.realsimple.com/home-organizing/cleaning/things-you-can-clean-in-dishwasher

Assignment:

Tip Applied:_____Date: _____
Tip Mastered: _____Date: _____

March 29

Time Management

Today is National Caffeine Awareness Day.

Homework

Save money by buying your favorite coffee, such as Starbucks, in the grocery store vs. Starbucks store. Keep extra bottles of soda at home too.

Other caffeine beverages:

- Sodas
- Tea
- Chocolate/cocoa
- Energy drinks

However, high doses of caffeine may have unpleasant and even dangerous side effects. Be careful how much caffeine you drink a day.

Assignment:

Tip Applied:_____Date: _____
Tip Mastered: _____Date: _____

March 30

Spirituality

"I can do all things through Him who strengthens me" (Philippians 4:13, ESV).

Homework

Many times, I didn't have the energy to complete a project or my chores. When I asked Jesus to give me strength, He did. Do you find yourself weak? Ask Jesus to give you strength and He will. He gave Samson miraculous strength.

Assignment:

Tip Applied:_____Date: _____
Tip Mastered: _____Date: _____

March 31

Charity

Deaf History Day is observed today.

The deaf like to be acknowledged as much as everyone else. It is vital to embrace those with disabilities.

Homework

Learn a little sign language so you can be friendly. You'll bless their hearts with a few hand signals of greeting.

Assignment:

Tip Applied:_____Date: _____
Tip Mastered: _____Date: _____

Chapter 4

April

"Then those who sing as well as those who play the flutes will say, 'All my springs of joy are in you'" (Psalm 87:7, NASB).

"Then a shoot will spring from the stem of Jesse, And a Branch from his roots will bear fruit" (Isaiah 11:1, NASB).

April 1

Laughter

April Fool's Day is a joke day.

There is a tradition of playing practical jokes and hoaxes on others. Play a practical joke on someone today.

Homework

Watching or listening to their response will make you laugh. It's my tradition to tell my husband that he has a flat tire every year! Every time he falls for it.

One time, when my granddaughter and I were in the vehicle, I told her to call her grandpa. Please tell him we just had two flat tires, and someone threw nails in the street. Two new tires were just purchased that had flat tires. He was surprised and was ready to pick us up. She responded, "April fools!" All of us laughed when we got him again!

Assignment:

Tip Applied:_____Date: _____
Tip Mastered: _____Date: _____

April 2

Etiquette

Send your RSVP promptly for parties and weddings.

Homework

Please respond as soon as possible to allow the host to prepare for your attendance. A delayed or disregarded RSVP appears unappreciative and inconsiderate.

Assignment:

Tip Applied:_____Date: _____
Tip Mastered: _____Date: _____

April 3

Organization & Time Management

Use a gym bag and pack all the toiletries, towels, clothes, water, and shoes you'll need for exercising and going to the gym.

Homework

Once it's packed, you can just grab the bag and go. You may want to store it in your vehicle. It is a beneficial push to be inspired to exercise, knowing you're all prepared to go.

Assignment:

Tip Applied:_____Date: _____
Tip Mastered: _____Date: _____

April 4

Charity & Etiquette

April is Alcohol Awareness month.

Alcohol addiction is publicized through this program. How often do you eat a meal with an alcoholic or recovering alcoholic?

Homework

The goal of this observance is to increase understanding of the causes of alcoholism and the available, effective treatments, as well as encouraging people that recovery is very possible. Refrain from taking possession of and / or offering any alcoholic beverages to them. This will keep them from becoming tempted.

Assignment:

Tip Applied:_____Date: _____
Tip Mastered: _____Date: _____

April 5

Organization

Do you have a large number of photos on your computer, phone, iPad, stick, or external hard drive?

Homework

All your photos that have duplicates are separated by the software. Also, the sources below are used by photo organizers to categorize your photos.

Sources:
Memory keeping solutions:
https://www.forever.com/

Full service for photos:
https://mylio.com/

Windows live gallery:
https://www.microsoft.com/en-us/p/live-gallery/9nsp371rs dr5#activetab=pivot:overviewtab

iPhoto's for Mac:
https://www.apple.com/macos/photos/

Assignment:

Tip Applied:_____Date: _____
Tip Mastered: _____Date: _____

April 6

Organization

My cellphone is missing. Where did I put it?

Homework

One option is to stand it up in a business card holder where it can be visible. It could be on a table, desk, counter, or somewhere else that is easy to find. Place it in a convenient location to be charged.

Assignment:

Tip Applied:_____Date: _____
Tip Mastered: _____Date: _____

April 7

Laughter

The Sunday School teacher was describing how Lot's wife looked back and turned into a pillar of salt, when little Jason interrupted, "My Mummy looked back once, while she was driving," he announced triumphantly, "and she turned into a telephone pole!"

A little boy got a new tie for his birthday. Sunday morning, he wore the new tie to church. He was so proud of his tie. He made sure everyone noticed it. Once the congregation settled down, the preacher approached the pulpit in preparation for the offering. The preacher said, "Now is the time we give back to the Lord. Please give your tithes (ties) and offerings to Christ." The little boy looked at his father and said, "Daddy, he wants my tie!"

Source:
https://www.Javacasa.com/humor/bible.htm

April 8

Spirituality & Charity

"And let us not grow weary of doing good, for in due season we will reap, if we do not give up" (Galatians 6:9, ESV).

Homework

You can feel unappreciated at times when you put in hard work every day. Press on, persevere, and remain faithful. You can be assured that Jesus sees it all, and His compensation is greater than man's.

Assignment:

Tip Applied:_____Date: _____
Tip Mastered: _____Date: _____

April 9

Time Management

Does your shopping routine include purchasing clothes without trying them on first?

Homework

Try them on before purchasing. You may find that they don't fit or look attractive on you. They may need to be returned to the store. If you cannot locate your receipt, you will have to stand in line again for a refund, money transaction, or price check. Trying clothes on before purchasing them is a time-saver.

Assignment:

Tip Applied:_____Date: _____
Tip Mastered: _____Date: _____

April 10

Organization

It's time to plant your flowers outdoors. Set up an assembly line of pots, dirt, flowers, and watering cans for gardening. Filling each pot will go much faster.

Homework

Once the pots are planted with flowers, you can place them on a stand, shepherd's hook, patio, or an area to make a decorative spot in the yard.

Assignment:

Tip Applied:_____Date: _____
Tip Mastered: _____Date: _____

April 11

Time Management & Organization

Are you a procrastinator? Do you let everyday things accumulate and pile up and say, "I'll deal with it later!?"

Homework

If you are overwhelmed and don't know where to start, or can't find something, you're in trouble. Develop a checklist that works. Begin a daily routine. You may need to force yourself to do it. Delayed decision-making can cause you to become or remain a procrastinator.

Assignment:

Tip Applied:_____Date: _____
Tip Mastered: _____Date: _____

April 12

Tip

House plants need water, fertilizer, sun, and TLC.

Homework

Give your plants the same amount of water each week, on the same day of the week. Only fertilize once a month, from spring to fall. The plants need to remain dormant during winter to spring. Measure, don't over-fertilize, otherwise the plants will burn and die.

Assignment:

Tip Applied:_____Date: _____
Tip Mastered: _____Date: _____

April 13

Laughter

My Italian uncle bought a new Cadillac convertible when they just came out and took all the nieces and nephews for a drive. When he went inside the house, he said, "Ma, I just bought this new car cheap, come outside and take a look at it." She took a look, and said in broken English, "No-a wonder it's a cheap-ed, it has-a no roof!"

Source:
Madeline and Dominic Allevato

April 14

Spirituality

"Delight yourself in the Lord, and He will give you the desires of your heart" (Psalm 37:4, ESV).

This scripture was engraved on our wedding invitations. Before receiving my heart's desire, I prayed for ten years that a godly man would come into my life. The Lord did just that! We have been celebrating our wedding anniversary since 1994.

Homework

Create a list of all the characteristics you desire in a husband and / or wife and stick to it.

Assignment:

Tip Applied:_____Date: _____
Tip Mastered: _____Date: _____

April 15

Organization

Are you a "filer" or a "piler" with paperwork?

Homework

If you're a piler:

- **Your allies are open bins and trays.** To keep items visible yet corralled, use stackable trays and wall or desktop racks. Bulletin boards and magnet boards help prevent essential notes and documents from getting lost.
- **The furniture you choose for your office should fit your style.** Open cubbies, credenzas, and console tables with bins are excellent choices. Portable carts are also a good option.
- **Visual cues can help you quickly locate what you are looking for.** There are several ways to do this, including color-coding or post-it notes in different colors. Consider investing in a label maker and label each folder, tray, or basket with its contents.

If you're a filer:

- **Take your file cabinet to the next level.** Use color-coded folders or clearly labeled file folders and organize them alphabetically or chronologically. Organize your papers into subgroups according to their content.
- **You may want to consider going digital.** Instead of holding on to hard copies, make your documents electronic, or scan and recycle them to save space and resources. For the piler, this simply wouldn't work—it's not visual

enough—but it's a perfect fit for the filer, who must keep everything neatly tucked away.

- **Remember to purge.** Make it a habit to go through your files once a quarter and shred or recycle anything you no longer need.

An organizer from SteelMaster keeps action items neat and easy to read. They are available at office supply stores.

Source:
https://www.hgtv.com/design/remodel/interior-remodel/are-you-a-piler-or-a-filer

Assignment:

Tip Applied:_____Date: _____
Tip Mastered: _____Date: _____

April 16

Organization

Online photo services have become the new trend. But what are you supposed to do with them?

Homework

For information on how to accomplish the task, check out the following websites.

- For print and photo gifts, visit Shutterfly
- For archiving and backing up, use SugarSync
- Photo sharing and photo prints can be purchased on Flickr

Source:
https://www.shutterfly.com/
https://www1.sugarsync.com/
https://www.flickr.com/explore

Assignment:

Tip Applied:_____Date: _____
Tip Mastered: _____Date: _____

April 17

Spirituality & Laughter

During the coronavirus pandemic, a priest from a parish in Grosse Pointe Park, Michigan, felt a need to see his members. As the vehicles were lined up in front of the parish, he started shooting a squirt gun with holy water to bless the people and their Easter baskets.

This is a true story. The priest was thinking out of the box and practicing social distancing. It was brilliant!

April 18

Charity

National Donate Life Day is celebrated today.

It is also celebrated throughout the month. The organization hosts several activities designed to encourage Americans to register as organ, eye, and tissue donors. It also honors those who have saved lives through their donations. You, too, can save lives.

Homework

You can apply to become an organ donor by visiting your state's Secretary of State Organ Donor Registry online. The donor form on the website can be completed in just one minute. You can either adhere the sticker to your driver's license and / or it will be printed on your new license. Share this with your family members so that many lives can be saved.

Source:
https://www.donatelife.net/thank-you-for-registration/

Assignment:

Tip Applied:_____Date: _____
Tip Mastered: _____Date: _____

April 19

Tip

This is National Couple Appreciation Day.

It reminds us to keep the flame of romance alive throughout the year. Do you remember the last time you went on a date with your spouse or significant other?

Homework

Spend time with your loved one and reconnect.

- Leave a love note on your mate's car.
- Surprise your love with coffee or tea before they wake up.
- If your sweetheart is a selfie-loving type and you're not, give in on occasion and take a couples' selfie.
- Let your significant other overhear you complimenting them. It's one thing for you to tell them directly, but to know you tell others what you think means so much more.
- Invite your love to go on an activity he or she enjoys. It doesn't need to be expensive. If they are always pestering you to go for a walk or to an event, they will be pleased by the gesture.
- Learn something new together such as a hobby, outdoor sports and so forth. Explore common interests where you both might have an opportunity to learn while spending time together and taking turns.

Put it on your calendar and go out to a movie, dinner, theatre, or event. Have some fun with each other!

Source:
https://nationaldaycalendar.com/national-couple-appreciation-month-april/

Assignment:

Tip Applied:_____Date: _____
Tip Mastered: _____Date: _____

April 20

Spirituality

"Jesus said to her, "'I am the resurrection and the life; the one who believes in Me will live, even if he dies, and everyone who lives and believes in Me will never die. Do you believe this?"' (John 11:25-26, NASB).

Homework

Attend church together as a family to worship the Lord Jesus Christ. Believe in Him so you can live with Him forever!

Assignment:

Tip Applied:_____Date: _____
Tip Mastered: _____Date: _____

April 21

Laughter

I once heard of a pastor who was offering a series of children's sermons on the symbols of the church. On one Sunday the pastor was speaking about pastoral clothing and asked the question, "Why do you think I wear this collar?" To this question came the response, "Because it kills fleas and ticks for up to five months."

Source:
https://www.javacasa.com/humor/sermon.htm

A little boy was attending his first wedding. After the service, his cousin asked him, "How many women can a man marry?" "Sixteen," the boy responded. His cousin was amazed that he knew the answer so quickly. "How do you know that?" "Easy," the little boy said. "All you have to do is add it up, like the Preacher said: 4 better, 4 worse, 4 richer, 4 poorer."

Source:
https://www.javacasa.com/humor/bible.htm

April 22

Organization

Is your purse so messy and cluttered that you cannot find anything in it?

Homework

Organize your wallet so it includes a coin purse, credit card slots, and pockets for gift cards. Use small, zippered pouches to store makeup, and use the pockets to hold pens, tissues, and other necessary items. Don't forget the money!

Assignment:

Tip Applied:_____Date: _____
Tip Mastered: _____Date: _____

April 23

Organization

Have the children help around the house. Match tasks to children's ages and abilities.

Homework

Plan a chore list, raise the bar, and don't be critical. Motivate them to earn rewards or allowance for being responsible and completing their jobs. Remember you are preparing them for the future.

Assignment:

Tip Applied:_____Date: _____
Tip Mastered: _____Date: _____

April 24

Organization

Create folders on your computer using File Explorer. Set up file categories for emails from certain people, companies, financial documents, lists, things to do, and projects.

Homework

File Explorer will help you find your documents faster. You can drag and drop items into these folders. Label the main folder generically and folders beneath more specifically. You can also click the name bar and it will alphabetize the files. Click the date modified bar above it and it will put it in recent order. You can find your documents faster.

Assignment:

Tip Applied:_____Date: _____
Tip Mastered: _____Date: _____

April 25

Tip

Spring cleaning and maintenance are essential.

Homework

Make sure the batteries, smoke alarms, and flashlights are working. Brush away ash from the fireplace. Consider hiring a chimney sweeper. Carpets should be shampooed, windows should be washed, and the cushions on the sofas vacuumed. You get the idea!

Assignment:

Tip Applied:_____Date: _____
Tip Mastered: _____Date: _____

April 26

Spirituality

"The next day he saw Jesus coming toward him, and said, 'Behold, the Lamb of God, who takes away the sin of the world!'" (John 1:29, ESV).

Homework

When we ask and pray to the Lord, He hears our prayers and forgives our sins.

Assignment:

Tip Applied:_____Date: _____
Tip Mastered: _____Date: _____

April 27

Laughter

"A father took his 5-year-old son to several baseball games where The Star-Spangled Banner was sung before the start of each game. Then the father and son attended a church on a Sunday shortly before Independence Day. The congregation sang The Star-Spangled Banner, and after everyone sat down, the little boy suddenly yelled out, 'PLAY BALL!!!'"

Source:
https://www.javacasa.com/humor/seasonal.htm

April 28

Tip

Flushing prescription medications down the toilet can cause them to seep and contaminate groundwater, surface waters, including rivers and lakes. Drinking water contaminated by these substances can end up in your body.

Homework

Consult your local government about nearby drug drop-offs and drug take-back programs. Alternatively, mix the medications with something inedible, such as coffee grounds, kitty litter, or dirt. Seal in a plastic bag to be thrown away.

Source:
https://www.fda.gov/consumers/consumer-updates/where-and-how-dispose-unused-medicines

Assignment:

Tip Applied:_____Date: _____
Tip Mastered: _____Date: _____

April 29

Organization

How do you handle business cards when someone hands them to you?

Homework

Using your smartphone, scan or snap a picture. You can search and store images with *CamCard* mobile phone app store. If you're a visual person, you might put the cards in a box or in a business cards plastic pages binder.

Assignment:

Tip Applied:_____Date: _____
Tip Mastered: _____Date: _____

April 30

Tip

It's Adopt-a-Shelter-Dog Day today.

Check with your local humane society or shelter to rescue a dog. If possible, wait to buy a dog from a breeder.

Homework

My Yorkie was rescued from a puppy mill where he had been subjected to abuse, trauma, depression, and loneliness. He was unloved and underweight. Now that I have him, he is happy and healthy. We adore each other, and he follows me everywhere I go in the house! Please rescue your best friend. Animals are a real blessing, especially during times of pandemic.

Assignment:

Tip Applied:_____Date: _____
Tip Mastered: _____Date: _____

Chapter 5

May

"Consider the lilies, how they grow: they neither labor nor spin; but I tell you, not even Solomon in all his glory clothed himself like one of these" (Luke 12:27, NASB).

May 1

Laughter

What does laughter do to your physical body?

- It stimulates many organs. Laughter enhances your intake of oxygen-rich air; stimulates your heart, lungs, and muscles; and increases the endorphins that are released by your brain.
- It activates and relieves your stress response. A rollicking laugh fires up and then cools down your stress response, and it can increase and then decrease your heart rate and blood pressure, resulting in a relaxed feeling.
- It soothes tension. Laughter can also stimulate circulation and aid muscle relaxation, both of which can help reduce the physical symptoms of stress.

Homework

Laughing exercises: use your diaphragm. This muscle in the body is attached to other muscles—abdominal, facial, respiratory, back, and legs—so laughing affects your whole body.

Long-term effects:

- **Improve your immune system**. Positive thoughts can release neuropeptides that help fight stress and potentially more-serious illnesses.
- **Relieve Pain**. Laughter may ease pain by causing the body to produce its own natural painkillers.
- **Increase personal satisfaction**. Laughter can also make it easier to cope with difficult situations.
- **Improve your mood**. Laughter can help lessen your stress, depression, anxiety, and improve self-esteem.

So, laugh!

Source:
https://www.mayoclinic.org/healthy-lifestyle/stress-management/in-depth/stress-relief/art-20044456

Assignment:

Tip Applied:_____Date: _____
Tip Mastered: _____Date: _____

May 2

Tip

This month, consider getting a massage. Take care of yourself. It's well deserved!

Homework

Multiple studies have shown the therapeutic value of a massage. Increased endorphins, serotonin, and dopamine are the processes in stimulating the autonomic nervous system. This helps increase levels of positive hormones within the body. Benefits include increased relaxation and decreased stress.

Source:
https://www.physio.co.uk/treatments/massage/index.php

Assignment:

Tip Applied:_____Date: _____
Tip Mastered: _____Date: _____

May 3

Spirituality

The National Day of Prayer falls during the first week of May.

"Hear my prayer, O Lord; give ear to my pleas for mercy! In your faithfulness answer me, in your righteousness!" (Psalm 143:1, ESV).

Spend time praying for families, friends, churches, schools, government leaders, other nations, and so forth.

Homework

The National Day of Prayer is an annual day of observance held on the first Thursday of May, designated by the United States Congress. People are asked "to turn to God in prayer and meditation." The president is required by law to sign a proclamation each year, encouraging all Americans to pray on this day.

Keep a prayer journal; include the date and the day when your prayers were answered. Whether it was yes, no, or wait, you'll find out when you pray.

Source:
https://en.wikipedia.org/wiki/National_Day_of_Prayer

Assignment:

Tip Applied:_____Date: _____
Tip Mastered: _____Date: _____

May 4

Laughter

True testimony:

The pastor invited everyone in the congregation who needed healing to come up for prayer. An older Italian man complained, "my-a stomach has-a been hurting, and I can't-a eat."

Three weeks later, giving his testimony, speaking from the pulpit, he said: "I came-a up for-a prayer for-a my stomach and I-a healed! "Now I-a can-a drink all-a the wine-a I-a want!"

May 5

Time Management

For approximately ten minutes, place permanent press garments in the dryer on the permanent-press cycle. One by one, shake each garment three times and hang it on a hanger to dry. Spray with a fabric softener spray and smooth out the front so it does not dry wrinkled. This will prevent the need to iron. Each time you remove a piece of clothing from the dryer, restart it.

Homework

Practice this technique to avoid ironing—it works!

- Refreshes fabrics
- Soothes away wrinkles
- Reduces static cling

Source:
https://downy.com/en-us/fabric-softener/wrinkle-spray/wrinkle-releaser

Assignment:

Tip Applied:_____Date: _____
Tip Mastered: _____Date: _____

May 6

Time Management

You should remove anything you wish to bring on the plane before you start boarding at the airport gate. You will find it convenient to take those items out before getting to your seat.

Homework

As an example, while at the gate waiting to board, remove your reading materials, water bottle, and earphones. When you reach your seat, there won't be enough time or space to dig through your carry-on.

Assignment:

Tip Applied:_____Date: _____
Tip Mastered: _____Date: _____

May 7

Time Management

When you are at the airport, keep a reusable water bottle with you and drink it before going through security. Make sure you drink the entire amount of water, or your bottle will have to be thrown out.

Homework

Refill your reusable water bottle after going through security. Many airports feature water fountains designed specifically for reusable water bottles. With more water available when needed, you'll save money and be happy you did!

Assignment:

Tip Applied:_____Date: _____
Tip Mastered: _____Date: _____

May 8

Organization

How long has it been since you organized your action paperwork on your desk?

Homework

Sort your papers according to project categories. Group them into piles and put them in the file folders according to their due dates. Place it in a tray or stand-up filing holder. Purge or shred what you don't need and then file in the filing cabinet.

Examples of red action file folders:

- Urgent
- Things to do
- Unpaid bills
- Follow up/Pending
- Filing

All these folders are on-going folders that you continually need and use. Once they are completed, then you can file or purge.

Assignment:

Tip Applied:_____Date: _____
Tip Mastered: _____Date: _____

May 9

Etiquette

How can manners help you influence others? Why is an RSVP necessary for a party? RSVP loosely translates from French as "Please Respond."

Homework

RSVP etiquette is one more way to show the host that you are honored to be included in their special day. They will be so pleased to know that you are making time for them.

Source:
https://www.etiquetteschoolofamerica.com/the-number-one-etiquette-violation-are-you-guilty-too/

Assignment:

Tip Applied:_____Date: _____
Tip Mastered: _____Date: _____

May 10

Spirituality

"For the word of God is living and active, sharper than any two-edged sword, even penetrating as far as the division of soul and spirit, of both joints and marrow, and able to judge the thoughts and intentions of the heart" (Hebrews 4:12, NASB).

Homework

Get into the habit of reading at least one chapter of the Bible daily. Record your devotions in a journal so that you can reference them later. Pass your journals on to your family and children. Aim to read the Bible in one year. Set this as your goal! If you don't finish it in a year, keep going until you do.

Assignment:

Tip Applied:_____Date: _____
Tip Mastered: _____Date: _____

May 11

Laughter

"The oldest computer can be traced back to Adam and Eve.

- It was an Apple
- But with extremely limited memory
- It was just one byte
- Then everything crashed"

Source:
https://www.Pleacher.com /chumor/humor/adameve.html

Computer humor:

- An **application** was for employment
- The **program** was a TV show
- A **cursor** used a swearword
- The **keyboard** was a piano!
- **Cut**—you did with a pocketknife
- **Paste**—you did with glue
- A **web** was a spider's home
- And the **virus** was the flu!

Source:
https://www.pleacher.com/chumor/miscmenu.html

May 12

Time Management

Get the best start to your day: rise early, take a shower, put on makeup, or shave, and get dressed.

Homework

Make sure you wake your children in time for them to get dressed, eat breakfast, get to school, and so forth. Some children find it very hard to wake up even if they get enough sleep. It is your challenge for the day not to be late.

Assignment:

Tip Applied:_____Date: _____
Tip Mastered: _____Date: _____

May 13

Organization

Where did you place your keys?

Homework

Place keys in the same place every day, so this becomes their "home." Hang keys on a hook by the door, place them on a table, or use a bowl. They sell magnetic key holders that you can put on a metal shelf in the garage if you forget your keys. Make sure the family immediately places the key holder back.

Assignment:

Tip Applied:_____Date: _____
Tip Mastered: _____Date: _____

May 14

Organization

Do you have a refrigerator door full of paperwork, photos, magnets, and schoolwork?

Homework

Rather than having a cluttered refrigerator door, create a binder that has tabs. Store all paperwork you frequently refer to in the binder. Have tabs for things like school, contacts, menus, to-dos, and so forth. Store it on a counter so it's always available. Clean out as needed.

Assignment:

Tip Applied:_____Date: _____
Tip Mastered: _____Date: _____

May 15

Organization

The process of moving requires changing your new address and keeping receipts for the moving expenses.

Homework

A month prior, acquire a USPS Change-of Address-Form from the post office or online. Change your address with your bank, friends, family, doctors, credit cards, utilities, and so forth. Ensure that all pertinent receipts are saved because moving expenses are typically tax deductible.

Source:
https://moversguide.usps.com/mgo/disclaimer

Assignment:

Tip Applied:_____Date: _____
Tip Mastered: _____Date: _____

May 16

Charity

When you have old towels and sheets, what do you do with them?

Homework

Donate to a charity, shelter for the homeless, or humane society. Your linen closet will be clutter free. Everyone will be blessed.

Assignment:

Tip Applied:_____Date: _____
Tip Mastered: _____Date: _____

May 17

Spirituality

"Keep your life free from love of money, and be content with what you have, for He has said, 'I will never leave you nor forsake you'" (Hebrews 13:5, ESV).

Homework

I thought I had done my best to hold onto my marriage, so when I was going through a divorce, I felt that I had sacrificed everything for it. My life was forever changed when Jesus said to me, "Put everything you have into me, and I will always be with you." I did just that, and it has transformed my life! It is amazing how just one scripture gives you faith and hope.

Assignment:

Tip Applied:_____Date: _____
Tip Mastered: _____Date: _____

May 18

Tip

Observe Military Appreciation Day today.

Observed on the third Saturday every May, this is a day dedicated to paying tribute to men and women currently serving in the U.S. Armed Forces. Take part in an activity with a military child.

Homework

Prepare a dad/mom board (vision board) that includes pictures, postcards, military patches, and a countdown calendar to count down the days until he/she returns from duty. The map should show where he or she is stationed. You can then add up the days! Pray for their safe return.

Assignment:

Tip Applied:_____Date: _____
Tip Mastered: _____Date: _____

May 19

Organization

What about the inside of your car? Does it get dirty? Has it become littered with trash, food particles, and clutter?

Homework

Everyone experiences it from time-to-time. If you have the car washed at a full-service or drive-through, remove any trash first, then have it vacuumed inside. Driving a car that's clean is a joy. It is recommended to wipe the steering wheel after eating and keep the wipes in the car. As you wipe, you should see dirt come off the steering wheel. Don't forget the mats need to be washed, especially from mud, snow, ice and so forth.

Assignment:

Tip Applied:_____Date: _____
Tip Mastered: _____Date: _____

May 20

Laughter

A mother and son had a discussion related to people living together these days, having premarital sex, and practicing it as a sport. According to her, they would have been stoned to death in biblical times. The son replied, "The Bible needs to be updated to reflect the current times."

His mother thought, "That was pointless."

May 21

Time Management

Do your eyes burn or feel strained from working on a computer for hours? Computer glasses may help to relieve digital eye strain; they can block or filter blue light from your screen. Time can reduce symptoms associated with digital eye strain, also known as computer vision syndrome.

Homework

Designed to reduce eye fatigue, the 20-20-20 rule says that every twenty minutes of screen time, you should look away at something at least twenty feet away for at least twenty seconds. These regular screen breaks give your eyes some much-needed rest to prevent eye strain.

Assignment:

Tip Applied:_____Date: _____
Tip Mastered: _____Date: _____

May 22

Organization

Everything has a designated place or "home." Keep like things together in their categories and homes.

Homework

Take small steps. Designate bins (plastic shoe boxes from the dollar store) in a dresser for socks, underwear, bras, nylons, and so forth. Donate belongings you don't need or use anymore. It feels good when you just make space and eliminate clutter.

Assignment:

Tip Applied:_____Date: _____

Tip Mastered: _____Date: _____

May 23

Tip

Rest is not laziness. Rest is building breaks into our lives before we collapse so we don't fall apart.

Homework

Make time for yourself first. Your mental, emotional, and spiritual health should be your top priority. Make time for family, community affairs, physical activities, and projects. Plan in advance but be flexible so you don't get stressed out. You may want to take a nap or relax with your feet up for fifteen minutes. Snack on something while you rest. You will feel refreshed and more productive afterward. This isn't the time to procrastinate with what you were doing. Get it done!

Assignment:

Tip Applied:_____Date: _____
Tip Mastered: _____Date: _____

May 24

Spirituality

"Do not give what is holy to dogs, and do not throw your pearls before pigs, or they will trample them under their feet, and turn and tear you to pieces" (Matthew 7:6, NASB).

Homework

Over and over again, have you given too much of yourself? Could others be taking advantage of you? Don't feel guilty if you've exhausted and sacrificed yourself while applying these biblical principles.

The word "pearls" is symbolic of godly wisdom and the salvation brought by His kingdom. God's wisdom is likened to something of a very great price. There are some people with whom you just cannot share the things of God. Such people will not respect those things. They will just mock them. You'll be trampled under their feet, and they will return to tear you apart.

Source:
https://www.studylight.org/commentary/matthew/7-6.html

Assignment:

Tip Applied:_____Date: _____
Tip Mastered: _____Date: _____

May 25

Time Management

How do you handle miscellaneous reading material and papers lying around your house?

Homework

Pick up what you don't need around the house or office. Keep what you need in a plastic envelope you can snap closed and keep in your vehicle or bag so you can read the items when you have extra time. If you are waiting for an appointment, make out your grocery list, next day's plans, phone calls, email, read, or pay your bills. Read while waiting in a doctor's office, bus, subway, waiting for someone, and so forth. Recycle, shred, or discard what you no longer need. Finding time like this can make all the difference in the world when it comes to your productivity level.

Assignment:

Tip Applied:_____Date: _____
Tip Mastered: _____Date: _____

May 26

Organization

Are you unsure of where to begin and what to do first in your home? There are many free online checklists available to help get your home organized and reduce clutter.

Homework

Search Better Homes & Gardens for free checklists on any topic related to household cleaning and organizing to beat clutter once and for all. Mark down the checklist and check off each item that you finished. Keep going until it is all completed. Then start the next checklist.

Source:
https://www.bhg.com/search/?q=checklists

Assignment:

Tip Applied:_____Date: _____
Tip Mastered: _____Date: _____

May 27

Organization

Organize weekly family meetings to discuss chores, homework, problems, meals, future plans, and so forth.

Homework

Rotating chore lists lets children select what chores they wish to do. Communicating with the family allows you to address any issues that may arise. Use the reward system and / or allowance.

Assignment:

Tip Applied:_____Date: _____
Tip Mastered: _____Date: _____

May 28

Etiquette

When dining at a table, elbow placement is important. The general etiquette of dining, along with manners these days seems lacking.

Homework

When you're not eating, you can place your elbows on the table. When you're eating, you can place your wrists on the table.

- Wash up and come to the table with clean hands.
- Remember to place your napkin on your lap.
- Chew with your mouth closed.
- Keep your smartphone off the table and set it to silent or vibrate.
- Hold and use utensils correctly.
- Wait to talk until you're done chewing to sip or swallow a drink.
- Say please to ask for things to be passed.
- Don't forget to give a compliment to the cook.

Assignment:

Tip Applied:_____Date: _____
Tip Mastered: _____Date: _____

May 29

Tip

Today is Fibromyalgia Education Day.

Fibromyalgia is a musculoskeletal disorder that causes chronic pain all over the body. It includes trigger points which when they are pressed are painful. I developed this chronic disease over twenty years ago. I took ibuprofen nearly every day for pain.

Homework

Use Tylenol instead. Chronic use of ibuprofen can lead to kidney damage. Mine reached stage three of kidney disease due to its regular use. I just want to give you a warning if you are experiencing the same symptoms.

Assignment:

Tip Applied:_____Date: _____
Tip Mastered: _____Date: _____

May 30

Laughter

"Being a new pastor to an aging congregation, I told them I would be serving them prune juice in Holy Communion. When asked why I would dare entertain such a thought, I said, 'If the Holy Spirit won't move you—the prune juice will!'"

Source:
https://www.javacasa.com/humor/pastor .htm

- Q. Where did the sheep want to go on vacation?
- A. To the baaahamas.

Source:
Unknown

May 31

Spirituality

Today is Memorial Day.

This national holiday was established to honor those who have died in American wars. Support your community by going to your local parade.

"But an opportunity came when Herod on his birthday gave a banquet for his nobles and military commanders and the leading men of Galilee" (Mark 6:21, ESV).

Homework

Military men and women serve our country and died for our freedom. We applaud military personnel when they march past at the parade. When you see a soldier, thank him or her for serving our country. Without them making sacrifices, we could be at war in America.

Assignment:

Tip Applied:_____Date: _____
Tip Mastered: _____Date: _____

Chapter 6

June

For behold, the winter is past,
The rain is over and gone.
The blossoms have already appeared in the land;
The time has arrived for pruning the vines,
And the voice of the turtledove has been heard in our land.
The fig tree has ripened its fruit,
And the vines in blossom have given forth their fragrance.
Arise, my darling, my beautiful one,
And come along! (Song of Solomon 2:11-15, NASB)

June 1

Spirituality

"For God so loved the world, that He gave His only Son, that whoever believes in Him shall not perish but have eternal life" (John 3:16, ESV).

Homework

This is a favorite scripture with hope and promises for everyone. By inviting Jesus Christ into your heart, the Bible says, you now have eternal life.

Assignment:

Tip Applied:_____Date: _____
Tip Mastered: _____Date: _____

June 2

Organization

Does your garage seem to be running out of space? An overhead rack might be the answer to your storage and organizational needs. In addition, you will gain more garage floor space.

Homework

Several companies manufacture overhead storage systems. The racks come in different dimensions, sizes, and designs to meet different weight requirements. All products are designed to meet safety and stability standards.

Source:
Amazon.com (type in "garage ceiling rack storage")

Assignment:

Tip Applied:_____Date: _____
Tip Mastered: _____Date: _____

June 3

Organization

By organizing tools and other items, you can sort your garage. In what part of the garage should these items go?

Homework

Having rails installed on the garage walls allows you to hang brooms, mops, shovels, rakes, bicycles, and so forth. By storing your items off the ground, you will gain easier access to them and have more storage space on the floor.

Assignment:

Tip Applied:_____Date: _____
Tip Mastered: _____Date: _____

June 4

Time Management

Are you able to find time for fun during the summer?

Homework

Prepare for summer by planning fun things to do and places to visit. Print out information from websites. Prepare a budget based on your travel time, gas, food, hotel costs, and so forth. Once that is determined, choose a day on the calendar, and get started!

Assignment:

Tip Applied:_____Date: _____
Tip Mastered: _____Date: _____

June 5

Tips

Disinfecting wipes are a fast and easy way to clean. The label tells you about specific germs the wipes can kill, e.g., the COVID-19 virus.

Homework

Disposable cleaning wipes contain a germ-killing solution. They're designed to kill viruses and bacteria on hard surfaces like doorknobs, counters, TV remotes, and phones. They don't work on soft surfaces like clothing or upholstery. Keep wipes in the kitchen and bathrooms to wipe off counters, sinks, toilets, and spills. It is quick, easy, and effective for COVID-19.

Source:
https://health.clevelandclinic.org/do-disinfecting-wipes-kill-the-coronavirus/

Assignment:

Tip Applied:_____Date: _____
Tip Mastered: _____Date: _____

June 6

Time Management

In addition to paying your bills, you should also save your tax receipts that you can claim.

Homework

Once you have paid business expenses, medical bills, utility bills, contributions, and other expenses, place the necessary documents in a tax folder. If your documents don't fall in that category, file them accordingly. All your documentation will be ready at tax time.

Assignment:

Tip Applied:_____Date: _____
Tip Mastered: _____Date: _____

June 7

Time Management

What methods do you use for keeping track of appointments and events, such as Franklin Planners, Day-Timers, and / or your cellphone calendar apps?

Homework

To keep track of your appointments, choose a method that works for you. There is no right or wrong way.

Assignment:

Tip Applied:_____Date: _____
Tip Mastered: _____Date: _____

June 8

Spirituality

"But Jesus said, 'Leave the children alone, and do not forbid them to come to Me; for the kingdom of heaven belongs to such as these'" (Matthew 19:14, NASB).

A child's prayer for grace:

"Tick-tock, tick-tock, now it's time to pray; we thank the Lord Jesus Christ for this meal today. Amen."

Source:
Troy Turner

June 9

Laughter

One day, a mother and son were riding a train together when the son asked, "Mom, don't preach today on the train." You do it everywhere we go." A man approached her and asked, "Is this aisle seat saved?" The mother said, "Funny you should say that; it is not saved yet!"

Source:
Debbie Tebbe

Q. What is so funny about forbidden fruits?
A. They create many jams.

Source:
https://christiancamppro.com/the-constantly-growing-list-of-funny-christian-jokes-with-pictures/

June 10

Organization

Place pictures or stickers on storage bins if your child is too young to read. You can teach them to put their toys and things away.

Homework

Purchase a ten-compartment storage unit; place stickers on each bin to indicate the type of toys in each compartment. Encourage your children to store toys according to the stickers they place on the bins. Remind them to "Put your toys in their home!" And where is that? Where it belongs.

Assignment:

Tip Applied:_____Date: _____
Tip Mastered: _____Date: _____

June 11

Organization

What is the best method for cleaning your Coach fabric purse when it becomes soiled?

Homework

Soak it in Oxi clean and laundry detergent for an hour. You will be amazed at the amount of dirt in the bottom of the sink. Wash it in the washing machine at low temperature on delicate. Take out and hang dry. This will make the purse clean and reusable. This method is not for everyone, so decide if you want to attempt it.

In fact, I considered throwing away my white coach fabric purse because it was so soiled. Therefore, I decided to put it in the washing machine. What did I have to lose? My surprise was that it became white again after washing and I sold it on eBay.

Assignment:

Tip Applied:_____Date: _____
Tip Mastered: _____Date: _____

June 12

Organization

Is there an office in your home? Utilize color-coded file folders, tray organizers, a filing cabinet, and basic office supplies to organize your desk.

Homework

When your office is organized, you can think more clearly and come up with a vision, plus creative and natural ideas. Make sure your desk is tidy when you are finished for the day.

Assignment:

Tip Applied:_____Date: _____
Tip Mastered: _____Date: _____

June 13

Organization

Organize your linen closet with plastic shoe boxes without lids. Label them individually. Examples of these are internal medications, external medications, soaps, hair products, dental care, and so forth.

Homework

Having label bins, you will know what you are running low on before heading to the store. There will be enough stock to take what you need at the moment. Furthermore, you will be able to locate what you need quickly. A well-organized closet or cupboard means that your family can easily take items out and put them back.

Assignment:

Tip Applied:_____Date: _____
Tip Mastered: _____Date: _____

June 14

Spirituality

"Honor your father and your mother, that your days may be long in the land that the Lord your God is giving you" (Exodus 20:12, ESV).

Homework

It is the fifth commandment. One day, you might be a mother or father, or you might be one right now. As we get older, we don't always agree with our parents, but we must respect them as God expects us to.

Assignment:

Tip Applied:_____Date: _____
Tip Mastered: _____Date: _____

June 15

Laughter

"When in doubt, panic!"
Just kidding! Take a deep breath, wait ten minutes, and then deal with the situation the best you can.

Source:
Chris Turner

A young boy sat with his teenage sister at Mass one Sunday. "What did you say," she asked him? "Busy, Busy, Boo," he said. "It is not Busy, Busy, Boo," she said. It is "Peace be with you."

Source:
https://www.javacasa.com/humor/miscell.htm

I lost my sixteen-year-old brother a couple months ago, and I explained Heaven to my three-year-old son that when you get to Heaven you can't return to earth. We were at my grandmother's house and my husband was using my grandmother's recliner that vibrated. When we were eating dinner, my husband told my stepdad that when he was in the recliner, he felt like he was in Heaven. My son looked at him and said, "You went to Heaven daddy? Why are you still here?"

Source:
https://www.javacasa.com/humor/bible.htm

June 16

Organization

Each family member should have a compartment or hook available in the mudroom or closet for storing their coat, hat, boots, scarf, backpack, and whatever else they need to hang up and keep together.

Homework

Teach family members to be more responsible by letting them hang up their coats and backpacks. Everything has a "home"! They will develop organizational skills to use in other aspects of their lives as well.

Assignment:

Tip Applied:_____Date: _____
Tip Mastered: _____Date: _____

June 17

Organization

Today, dolls come with an extensive wardrobe. Repurpose travel toiletry cases into portable closets for doll clothes, accessories, shoes, and so forth.

Homework

Children should play with a single toy or activity at a time. Having too many items out will cause parts to be spread out and possibly get lost. Additionally, you could step on the pieces, and they can break or hurt your feet. Sorting, picking up, and putting them away will save much time.

Assignment:

Tip Applied:_____Date: _____
Tip Mastered: _____Date: _____

June 18

Organization

Gather materials together for scrapbooking and / or inserting photos before getting started with your craft.

Homework

Before gluing, sketch or lay out your ideas, pages, and techniques. Organize all your paper scraps, photos, and items in plastic photo containers or albums, and label them for easy-viewing and storage.

Assignment:

Tip Applied:_____Date: _____
Tip Mastered: _____Date: _____

June 19

Organization

Create a well-organized and safe storage plan for children's toys. Depending on their ages, toy boxes can vary in size.

Homework

Large toy boxes can be dangerous, as children may fall in to retrieve a toy! Toys can be put away more easily without a lid on the toy box when children are cleaning up. Children should pick up their toys before going to bed.

Assignment:

Tip Applied:_____Date: _____
Tip Mastered: _____Date: _____

June 20

Tip

When packing for travel, safeguard liquid toiletries by wrapping items in Ziploc bags.

Homework

It will avoid spills and other suitcase disasters when traveling. Remember only three ounces or less can go in your carry-on suitcase when flying. You may already know this, but it never hurts to be reminded.

Assignment:

Tip Applied:_____Date: _____
Tip Mastered: _____Date: _____

June 21

Spirituality

"But about that day and hour no one knows, not even the angels of heaven, nor the Son, but the Father alone. For the coming of the Son of Man will be just like the days of Noah" (Matthew 24:36-37, NASB).

Homework

If anyone asks you when Jesus is coming back for you, no one knows, not even Jesus. Only God knows! When faithful Christians are taken to heaven in a blink of an eye, it is called the Rapture. Non-Christians will be left on this earth to survive without them. The situation could be compared to hell on earth. Pray and ask Jesus into your heart right now!

Assignment:

Tip Applied:_____Date: _____
Tip Mastered: _____Date: _____

June 22

Laughter

"Three ministers were discussing the problem of bats in the attic at church and how difficult they were to get rid of. The first minister said that his congregation had tried smoking them out, but they still came back. Another had tried poisoning them, but enough survived to repopulate the attic. The third minister shared his solution: 'I just baptized and confirmed them all, and they NEVER came back!'"

Source:
https://www.javacasa.com/humor/sermon.htm

My son said after the offering one Sunday: "God must be poor to be always needing our money!"

Source:
https://www.javacasa.com/humor/bible.htm

June 23

Organization

A study conducted by the University of California, Los Angeles, concluded that three out of four American families can't park their vehicles in the garage due to clutter. The researchers found that "cars have been banished from seventy-five percent of garages to make way for rejected furniture and cascading bins and boxes of mostly forgotten household goods."

Homework

A cluttered garage also creates a dangerous fire hazard and will need a potential escape route. Categorize items, donate what you don't need, and label items. Place tools on shelves and walls. Storage can be on the ceiling in the garage too. Throw away what is broken. Then you can find your items, park in the garage, and be safe. Additionally, it causes wear and tear on the vehicle to be left outside unprotected.

Source:
http://magazine.ucla.edu/features/the-clutter-culture/index1.html

Assignment:

Tip Applied:_____Date: _____
Tip Mastered: _____Date: _____

June 24

Organization

Need a photo organizer?

Homework

A range of services are provided, including digital photo books, digital photo slide shows, printed photo organizers, traditional photo albums, custom framing, scanner services, cloud storage, and archival products.

Source:
https://thephotomanagers.com/hire-a-pro/

Assignment:

Tip Applied:_____Date: _____
Tip Mastered: _____Date: _____

June 25

Tip

Is your vehicle periodically maintained?

Homework

Rotating your tires is recommended every six to eight thousand miles. The wheel alignment and balance of your tires should be checked by a tire dealer. Make sure your spare tire is always ready to go by checking the air pressure in case of a flat. Be sure to keep your oil changes and tune-ups according to schedule.

Assignment:

Tip Applied:_____Date: _____
Tip Mastered: _____Date: _____

June 26

Tip

Where do you place greetings and holiday cards you get in the mail? They are expensive, along with the postage, and should be displayed, at least for a week.

Homework

Do you place greeting cards on your mantle, refrigerator, table, counter, or tape them on a window? After displaying, pick special cards from your immediate family to save in a memorabilia box and recycle the rest.

Assignment:

Tip Applied:_____Date: _____
Tip Mastered: _____Date: _____

June 27

Etiquette

Etiquette for planes, buses, and trains:

Homework

- On a plane, the person in the middle seat gets both armrests because they don't have the aisle armrest or the window to lean on. When flying, you need the armrests in the middle to sit comfortably.
- Bus etiquette would be to get up from your seat and let an elderly person, mother with a baby, or a disabled person have your seat.
- Traveling by train can be a lot of fun. On the train, you can walk around and have a meal in the dining car. They have tables in the seating area for computer work, games, reading and / or eating.

Assignment:

Tip Applied:_____Date: _____
Tip Mastered: _____Date: _____

June 28

Spirituality

"For the husband is the head of the wife even as Christ is the head of the church, His body, and is Himself its Savior" (Ephesians 5:23, ESV).

Homework

You will see blessings upon your family as you pray and spend time in His Word. Begin having family devotions and attend church together as a family. This is an example you can give your children and family members. Managing your family and household is both honorable and respectable.

Assignment:

Tip Applied:_____Date: _____
Tip Mastered: _____Date: _____

June 29

Laughter

"A cat died and went to heaven. At the gate, he told God how he had been abused all his life on earth. God told him he is going to make his life very comfortable in heaven. The next day, six mice came to heaven. They gave God a similar story about their hard life on earth—because cats were constantly chasing them. God told them he'll make their life very comfortable. They asked that he give them skates so they wouldn't be running anymore. God granted their request. A week later God was passing by and found the cat comfortably resting. He asked the cat how things were going. The cat said, 'Oh wonderful, God, those meals on wheels that you have been sending me are delicious!'"

Source:
https://javacasa.com/humor/pearlygate.htm

June 30

Tip

Follow the directions on how much laundry soap, bleach, fabric softener, and Oxi Clean to use. Using too much can cause your washing machine to overflow.

Homework

Prepare little cups or containers that are the right size for measuring and pouring. Follow the directions to the washer compartments and drawer. There are little pods such as laundry soap that are convenient and a safe amount to use.

Assignment:

Tip Applied:_____Date: _____
Tip Mastered: _____Date: _____

Chapter 7

July

But the fruit of the Spirit is love, joy, peace, patience, kindness, goodness, faithfulness, gentleness, self-control; against such things there is no law. And those who belong to Christ Jesus have crucified the flesh with its passions and desires. (Galatians 5:22-24, NASB)

July 1

Charity

Are you an impulsive buyer and like nice things even though you don't need the items or can't afford them?

Homework

Ask yourself these questions next time you go shopping and pick up an item you want to buy:

- Do I need it or want it?
- How many of these do I already have?
- When was the last time I used it?
- Where will I put it?

If you answered yes to even one of these questions, ask yourself if you should buy it. Maybe now is the time to make some serious changes.

Assignment:

Tip Applied:_____Date: _____
Tip Mastered: _____Date: _____

July 2

Etiquette

What do you say after someone passes away? "I know what you're going through."

Homework

It is better not to say that unless you have experienced it yourself as it may offend them. During their time of loss, you can say, "I'm sorry for your loss," or "I offer you my deepest condolences," or "I will continue to pray for you and the family," as you give them a warm hug. Sending a sympathy card would be thoughtful.

Assignment:

Tip Applied:_____Date: _____
Tip Mastered: _____Date: _____

July 3

Time Management

Are you on your way to a road trip or about to start your vacation?

Homework

Be sure to pack plenty of water, snacks, chargers / headphones for all electronics, games, sunglasses, sunscreen, pillows, blankets, first aid kits, hats, and trash bags. This is your time to bond as a family. Enjoy the adventure since you're all set!

Assignment:

Tip Applied:_____Date: _____
Tip Mastered: _____Date: _____

July 4

Tip

Why do we celebrate the Fourth of July and what does it mean?

Homework

A Fourth of July celebration brings together family and friends for picnics, fireworks, parades, and patriotism. In the United States, it commemorates the Declaration of Independence with freedom.

Assignment:

Tip Applied:_____Date: _____

Tip Mastered: _____Date: _____

July 5

Organization

What is the best way to organize all the memorabilia your family collects? Should you keep all the awards, trophies, and paperwork as they get older?

Homework

You don't want memorabilia to grow ten containers tall! Choose one suitable container per person and fill it with items and memories that are dear to you. You may be surprised that your children don't want the items anymore. Ask yourself, who am I saving it for?

Assignment:

Tip Applied:_____Date: _____
Tip Mastered: _____Date: _____

July 6

Spirituality

"Cast your burden on the Lord, and He shall sustain you; He shall never permit the righteous to be moved" (Psalm 55:22, ESV).

Homework

Are you worried about a lot of things and feeling heavily burdened? Pray to Jesus to ease your burdens, and He will. Your problems should be placed in the palm of your hands and laid at the cross. Walk away without looking back and don't pick them up again! In faith, it works.

Assignment:

Tip Applied:_____Date: _____
Tip Mastered: _____Date: _____

July 7

Time Management & Organization

Do you enjoy playing cards?

Homework

After picking up your hand of cards to play, lay out the cards face down that you will play at your next turn. If you do this, the other players won't have to wait for you. It makes the time more pleasant to play.

Assignment:

Tip Applied:_____Date: _____
Tip Mastered: _____Date: _____

July 8

Organization & Charity

For many people, cleaning out closets can be an overwhelming task. Here are a few tips.

Homework

Once a year, clean out all your closets so things don't stack up. Label the boxes and / or plastic bags with "charity," "consignment," "keep," and "purge." Place the "keep" pieces back where they belong. Once you have everything organized, head to your local consignment store. Those items they don't take, as well as anything labeled "charity," can be delivered to a local charity.

Assignment:

Tip Applied:_____Date: _____
Tip Mastered: _____Date: _____

July 9

Organization

The month of July is ideal for garage sales and yard sales.

Homework

Using the "Garage sale checklist," you'll find step-by-step instructions for organizing a garage sale. Depending on your city, you may need a permit. A plan will help you achieve better results.

Sources:

https://www.moving.com/tips/throwing-a-garage-sale-use-this-foolproof-checklist/

Assignment:

Tip Applied:_____Date: _____
Tip Mastered: _____Date: _____

July 10

Organization

What is the best way to organize the items for a garage sale?

Homework

- Categorize similar items together in a single area.
- You can place large items such as furniture, along the driveway to draw attention. Angle your furniture to make it look more appealing. You want cars and people walking by to stop and look which will entice them to come in.
- Make sure everything has a price tag. Dollar stores sell stickers with prices already written on them.
- Having a great presentation is very important.
- Know your prices so that you are not overcharging or undercharging.
- Check prices prior to selling any piece that is a designer item or from a collection, so you can get its full value.

Source:
https://unclutteredsimplicity.com/stress-free-yard-sale-tips/

Assignment:

Tip Applied:_____Date: _____
Tip Mastered: _____Date: _____

July 11

Tip

Is there anything left over from the garage sale that is worth the money?

Homework

Visit the consignment shop if you want to sell items. eBay and Facebook Marketplace are also great places to sell something. You'll at least get some money from them. Donate the item to charity if it doesn't sell.

Assignment:

Tip Applied:_____Date: _____
Tip Mastered: _____Date: _____

July 12

Laughter

Nicholas asked his dad, "How come I have so many names?" His dad said, "What do you mean, Nick?" "Well, some people call me 'Nick-olas,' and some people call me 'Nick.' Aunt Janet calls me 'Nickle-Pickle,' and my big cousins call me 'Nick-ster.'"

So, his dad said, without really thinking, "Those are Nick-names!"

Source:
Dr. Janet Blakely

July 13

Spirituality

"But seek first the kingdom of God and his righteousness, and all these things will be added to you. "Therefore, do not be anxious about tomorrow, for tomorrow will be anxious for itself. Sufficient for the day is its own trouble" (Matthew 6:33-34, ESV).

Homework

Seek God first to receive an answer for direction. You need to stay on His path, so you are within His will.

Assignment:

Tip Applied:_____Date: _____
Tip Mastered: _____Date: _____

July 14

Tip

Are you a procrastinator when it comes to exercise?

Homework

Begin by setting small, reachable goals. Rather than saying, "I am going to lose weight," tell yourself, "I am making myself healthy." This will prevent disappointment if you fail to achieve it. It is recommended to exercise 150 minutes per week. Don't forget to drink plenty of water. It is recommended to drink half your weight in ounces.

Assignment:

Tip Applied:_____Date: _____
Tip Mastered: _____Date: _____

July 15

Time Management

Have you ever heard of the amenities available to babies at hotels? Travel tips and checklists are also available.

Homework

Baby cribs, highchairs, and safety gates are available. The hotel will deliver diapers, formula, and other essentials to your room instead of you packing them. You can also order from Amazon Prime, which provides free delivery. This can help you save on baggage fees at the airport, plus carrying all the supplies.

Source:
https://havebabywilltravel.com/baby-supplies-shipping/

Assignment:

Tip Applied:_____Date: _____
Tip Mastered: _____Date: _____

July 16

Tip

Have you heard of the bin theory? It is what professional organizers practice and use to help clients declutter.

Homework

Start with bins, large plastic bags and / or baskets, each with one of the following labels: KEEP, DONATE, PURGE, SHRED, RECYCLE and CONSIGNMENT. Begin with a room and pick up one item at a time and put it in the properly labeled bin. Keep going until the room is free of clutter. Take proper action with each bin as to where to redistribute the contents.

Assignment:

Tip Applied:_____Date: _____
Tip Mastered: _____Date: _____

July 17

Tip

You should check your receipts from supermarkets before you leave the store. They could charge you a regular price for an item, especially if it was on sale. Once you're there you can handle the refund. When arriving home throw receipts away. Save all your receipts from other stores in a file for a possible return. Be sure to clean out the file every month. To claim those receipts for the upcoming year, place them in your tax folder if you have a home business and / or you can claim them on a long form.

Homework

Going shopping can result in receipts piling up. Save the receipt only if there is a possibility of a return. The retailer is cracking down heavily on returns. Your returned item may be refunded at the lowest selling price, you may receive store credit, or you may get no refund.

Assignment:

Tip Applied:_____Date: _____
Tip Mastered: _____Date: _____

July 18

Tip

You are not the only person who struggles with stress-eating. Food often provides comfort during stressful times. We enjoy eating it because it smells delicious, tastes delightful, and makes us feel good in the moment. Eating habits are a way for people to avoid dealing with their underlying emotions. Overeating makes you feel guilty and ashamed, which contributes to your underlying emotions. Overeating is a destructive cycle.

Homework

Emotional eaters may find that dieting does not work. To break the chain of emotional overeating for good, you need to break ingrained behaviors and address the root cause of emotional overeating. There is therapy available to help you get over that hump. Hopefully this will offer you a spark of faith to persevere.

Source:
https://www.getsupporti.com/for/stress-eating

Assignment:

Tip Applied:_____Date: _____
Tip Mastered: _____Date: _____

July 19

Laughter

Q. What kind of motor vehicles are in the Bible?
A. Jehovah drove Adam and Eve out of the Garden of Eden in a Fury. David's Triumph was heard throughout the land. The apostles were all in one Accord.

Q. What kind of lights did Noah use on the ark?
A. Flood lights

Q. What kind of car does Jesus' drive?
A. A Christ-ler.

Source:
https://javacasa.com/humor/bible.htm

July 20

Spirituality

"Jesus answered him, 'Truly, truly, I say to you, unless one is born again, he cannot see the kingdom of God.' Nicodemus said to him, 'How can a man be born when he is old? Can he enter a second time into his mother's womb and be born?' Jesus answered, 'Truly, truly, I say to you, unless one is born of water and the Spirit, he cannot enter the kingdom of God'" (John 3:3-5, ESV).

Homework

How does someone become a born-again believer? Simply ask Jesus into your heart. By repenting of sins known to you, you will allow the Holy Spirit to come and live within you. That empty hole in your heart will be filled.

Assignment:

Tip Applied:_____Date: _____
Tip Mastered: _____Date: _____

July 21

Charity

In your closet, keep a bag or box for charity donations.

Homework

If you don't put items into the bag or box when you're done with them, then you'll probably keep them. Donate them to a local charity when full. Make sure you get a tax receipt.

Assignment:

Tip Applied:_____Date: _____
Tip Mastered: _____Date: _____

July 22

Organization

Take things up or down, to the place where they belong.

Homework

Toys, shoes, or any other item that needs to be taken up or down the stairs can be stored in a decorative basket on the bottom step. Everyone should go through the basket for their items and put them away. It is important that you do not put so many belongings on the stairs that you can't walk on them. Make sure everything is put away in its "home."

Assignment:

Tip Applied:_____Date: _____
Tip Mastered: _____Date: _____

July 23

Tip

In high traffic areas, it is possible to prevent the carpet from wearing out or becoming dirty.

Homework

- Lay decorative throw rugs and runners on top of the carpet.
- Those can be washed when dirty to keep the carpet nice and clean.
- Vacuum regularly to keep the carpet clean.
- Vinegar and water solution create an acetic acid, which is capable of killing bacteria and removing dirt from carpets while freshening them up.
- Make your own vinegar-based stain remover and spot cleaner by mixing one part vinegar with two parts lukewarm water in a spray bottle.
- Do not wait; clean up spills and dirt as soon as possible.
- Rent a carpet cleaner if you can't afford to get a carpet cleaning service.

Assignment:

Tip Applied:_____Date: _____
Tip Mastered: _____Date: _____

July 24

Time Management

When storing pantyhose, bras, silky underwear, and other delicate items, use a small delicate mesh bag to prevent snags, runs, and rips. Place it in your washing machine on delicate—pantyhose rarely run when washed in this method.

Homework

To use in the washing machine, purchase a mesh laundry bag with a zipper. Machine-washing delicate items in this bag will save time from handwashing them.

Assignment:

Tip Applied:_____Date: _____
Tip Mastered: _____Date: _____

July 25

Tip

Prepare a special day to remember for your children. This is a really cool idea for their birthday. Let your imagination run wild! It'll be a day they'll never forget!

Homework

Provide lunches to fill the tackle boxes for kids to enjoy while camping, swimming, or at the beach. Serve your little one's chocolate pudding with cookie "dirt" and gummy bears. Set your table with splashes of aquatic colors and fishbowl centerpieces to give it an underwater feel.

Assignment:

Tip Applied:_____Date: _____
Tip Mastered: _____Date: _____

July 26

Spirituality

"Remember the Sabbath day, to keep it holy." Six days you shall labor, and do all your work, but the seventh day is a Sabbath to the Lord your God. On it you shall not do any work" (Exodus 20:8, ESV).

Homework

This is the fourth commandment. Attend church, then have lunch with family or friends as a tradition. Afterward, retire to your home and rest. Have a quiet nap and rejuvenate yourself.

Assignment:

Tip Applied:_____Date: _____
Tip Mastered: _____Date: _____

July 27

Laughter

Q. Who was the first person with a tablet downloading data from the cloud?

A. Technically, Moses

Source:
https://www.pleacher.com/chumor/humor/moses.html

One beautiful Sunday morning, a pastor announced to his congregation: "My good people, I have here in my hands three sermons. A $1000 sermon that lasts five minutes, a $500 sermon that lasts fifteen minutes, and a $100 sermon that lasts a full hour. Now, we'll take the collection and see which one I'll deliver."

Source:
https://www.javacasa.com/humor/sermon.htm

July 28

Time Management

Studies have shown that people lose significant time each day due to disorganization when they can't find a document.

Homework

Gather all loose papers, old magazines, old brochures, catalogs, and receipts with a plastic container or basket as you walk through your office. Organize them into piles and decide what to keep, shred, and what to throw away. File what you have left over. Once you get started, you will see that what you have left is not overwhelming.

Assignment:

Tip Applied:_____Date: _____
Tip Mastered: _____Date: _____

July 29

Organization

In the event of people moving and / or acquiring a new phone number and address, how do you manage it?

Homework

The information can be entered into your smartphone contacts or added to your address book. It is important to record the information as soon as possible because it will accumulate quickly.

Assignment:

Tip Applied:_____Date: _____
Tip Mastered: _____Date: _____

July 30

Time Management

Take fifteen minutes to power clean every day.

Homework

Play a game with your children by cleaning their rooms, putting their toys away, and wiping down the bathroom with wipes. Put on dance music, set a timer, and see who finishes first. The winner gets a reward, perhaps a snack.

Assignment:

Tip Applied:_____Date: _____
Tip Mastered: _____Date: _____

July 31

Tip

There's nothing worse than having insects in or outside your house, so here are some tips.

Homework

- Make a nontoxic repellent by mixing equal amounts of white vinegar and water into a spray bottle. This is safe for use on floors, baseboards, and crevices. You can even use it outside!
- All types of bugs, including fleas and ants, can be removed with Palmolive dish soap, too. If the inside or outside of your house is infested with bugs, spray a Palmolive and water mixture along the foundation and /or under the baseboards. It works effectively against roaches, wasps, moths, spiders, and more. The product is safe for use on fruits, vegetables, and garden plants.

I recall my grandfather growing fruits and vegetables in his own garden in the 1960s. Since there were no bug killer sprays back then, he used Palmolive soap. It is safe to use on food to eat. Thank God, it worked!

Fact: The Palmolive company created bars of soap in 1894, when it was founded.

Source:
https://moviecultists.com/can-palmolive-be-used-on-plants

Assignment:

Tip Applied:_____Date: _____
Tip Mastered: _____Date: _____

Chapter 8

August

"In My Father's house are many rooms; if that were not so, I would have told you, because I am going there to prepare a place for you.

And if I go and prepare a place for you, I am coming again and will take you to Myself, so that where I am, there you also will be" (John 14:2-3, NASB).

August 1

Organization

Today, people receive an abundance of mail and often do not know how to sort it.

Homework

- Bring in the stack from the mailbox. Separate junk mail from important mail.
- Separate bills that need to be paid.
- Place magazines and coupons in two piles.
- Sort the remaining important mail by each person in the home. It's their responsibility to pick up their mail and handle it.

Assignment:

Tip Applied:_____Date: _____

Tip Mastered: _____Date: _____

August 2

Laughter

When you laugh and smile with someone, the instinctive response is to look directly in their eyes.

Homework

Smiling is universally identified as a sign of happiness. Laughing together is as close as you can get to a hug without touching.

Assignment:

Tip Applied:_____Date: _____
Tip Mastered: _____Date: _____

A three-year-old girl was getting ready to graduate from pre-school. So, she told her mother that she was going to make a speech at the graduation. Her mother said to her "You know what will happen after you graduate?" Her response was, "I GOTTA GET A JOB, RIGHT MOM?"

Source:
https://www.javacasa.com/humor/reallife.htm

August 3

Spirituality

"No, in all these things we are more than conquerors through Him who loved us" (Romans 8:37, ESV).

Homework

When you feel defeated, just say over and over again, "I am more than a conqueror in Christ Jesus." It will give you hope, self-worth, and build up your self-esteem.

Assignment:

Tip Applied:_____Date: _____
Tip Mastered: _____Date: _____

August 4

Organization

If you own a business and need to keep receipts for expenses, try this.

Homework

You can put the receipts in your purse, wallet, or vehicle. Store them in a plastic snap-shut envelope and take them out when you arrive at home and / or office. Prepare your receipts for the tax season by sorting and categorizing them, placing them in the tax folder for next year, and / or completing a work-related expense report.

Assignment:

Tip Applied:_____Date: _____
Tip Mastered: _____Date: _____

August 5

Etiquette

Keep a Ziploc bag handy for dirty diapers when changing a baby in a public place or someone's home. This way there won't be a stinky smell left behind.

Homework

Be sure to keep Ziploc bags in your diaper bag and purse. You should be discreet when changing the baby's diaper and disposing of it in the trash.

Assignment:

Tip Applied:_____Date: _____
Tip Mastered: _____Date: _____

August 6

Organization & Time Management

Parents can store children's outfits in the compartment stacker for the week. Each child will find their clothes and shoes in the organized stacker in the closet for that day. It will save them a great deal of time!

Homework

Your children need to be responsible for getting dressed every morning with their entire outfit already picked out—including their shoes.

Assignment:

Tip Applied:_____Date: _____
Tip Mastered: _____Date: _____

August 7

Organization

How long should you keep cosmetics before throwing them out?

Homework

- Replace mascara every three months.
- Water-based products and foundation last a year and oil-based products for eighteen months.
- Powders, eyeshadows, and blushes are good for two years.
- Replace cream shadows every 9-12 months.
- Replace lipsticks every year.
- Use a makeup brush cleanser frequently for your makeup brushes.
- You can clean or wipe cosmetics with rubbing alcohol to disinfect them.

Assignment:

Tip Applied:_____Date: _____
Tip Mastered: _____Date: _____

August 8

Spirituality

"Love is patient, love is kind, it is not jealous; love does not brag, it is not arrogant. It does not act disgracefully, it does not seek its own benefit; it is not provoked, does not keep an account of a wrong suffered, it does not rejoice in unrighteousness, but rejoices with the truth; it keeps every confidence, it believes all things, hopes all things, endures all things.

But now faith, hope, and love remain, these three; but the greatest of these is love" (1 Corinthians 13:4-7, 13, NASB).

Homework

Remember to kiss and hug your family members every day before you leave the house, because you never know when it could be the last time. The love chapter also includes unconditional love, so love with all your heart.

Assignment:

Tip Applied:_____Date: _____

Tip Mastered: _____Date: _____

August 9

Laughter

"A wealthy man died and went to heaven. He was met at the Pearly Gates by Saint Peter who led him down the streets of gold. They passed mansion after mansion until they came to the very end of the street. Saint Peter stopped the rich man in front of a little shack. 'This belongs to you,' said Saint Peter.

'Why do I get this ugly thing when there are so many mansions I could live in?' demanded the man.

'We did the best we could with the money you sent us!' Saint Peter replied."

Source:
https://javacasa.com/humor/pastor.htm

August 10

Time Management

Do as much as you can today rather than putting it off until tomorrow. Get your emails read, phone calls, chores done, run errands, and so forth. Tomorrow will be just as busy but look at all you accomplished today.

Homework

There are only twenty-four hours in a day, so let's catch up today. Perhaps there will be time to do other things later and put up your feet and rest with a good book.

Assignment:

Tip Applied:_____Date: _____
Tip Mastered: _____Date: _____

August 11

Organization

Marie Kondo wrote a book called "*Spark Joy.*" Marie Kondo is Japanese and an organizing genius. Being organized will help more people live a life that sparks joy in their lives. The tools and services she offers are designed to help you get there using the simplest, most effective tools and methods.

Homework

As an example, she tells people to take all their clothes out of closets, drawers, and other places. Pick up each item and ask yourself, "Is it bringing me joy? Keep it. If not, say thank you, and donate it. If you use this approach, you'll get rid of more clothes than expected.

Source:
https://konmari.com/

Assignment:

Tip Applied:_____Date: _____
Tip Mastered: _____Date: _____

August 12

Organization

Are you having a hard time getting rid of gifts and memorabilia that were given to you?

Homework

Ask yourself the following questions:

- How long have you had it?
- When was the last time you used it?
- Did you enjoy it?
- How many of the gifts you gave others are still being used or are still in their possession?
- Take a picture and move on.

Maybe they no longer have your gift after so many years. It is time to stop feeling guilty.

Assignment:

Tip Applied:_____Date: _____
Tip Mastered: _____Date: _____

August 13

Spirituality

"Children, obey your parents in the Lord, for this is right. 'Honor your father and mother' (this is the fifth commandment), 'that it may go well with you and that you may live long in the land.' Fathers, do not provoke your children to anger, but bring them up in the discipline and instruction of the Lord" (Ephesians 6:1-3 ESV).

Homework

When my children were little and misbehaved, I had them quote this scripture. They knew it by heart because I said it to them so many times. They straightened up because they knew it was the right thing to do.

Assignment:

Tip Applied:_____Date: _____
Tip Mastered: _____Date: _____

August 14

Organization

Shoe boxes make excellent storage containers if you want to be economical. Wrap the boxes in colorful paper like a gift, paint, or paint the covers with decoupage paste for a long-lasting finish.

Homework

You can ask friends and / or a shoe store for their shoeboxes or save your own. Repurposing and staying organized is another reason. They can be reused in so many different ways.

Assignment:

Tip Applied:_____Date: _____
Tip Mastered: _____Date: _____

August 15

Laughter

"A teenager had just gotten his driving permit. He asked his father about the use of the car. His father said to him, 'I'll make a deal with you. You bring your grades up, study your Bible, get your hair cut, and we'll talk about it.'

After a week the boy came back and asked his father about the car. 'Son, I've been really proud of you. You have brought your grades up, you've studied your Bible diligently, but you didn't get your hair cut!'

The son replied, 'But Dad, Samson had long hair, Moses had long hair, Noah had long hair, and even Jesus had long hair.' His father replied, 'Yes, and they WALKED everywhere they went!'"

Source:
https://www.javacasa.com/humor/pearlygate.htm

August 16

Spritualty

"See what kind of love the Father has given to us that we should be called children of God; and so, we are. The reason why the world does not know us is that it did not know him" (1 John 3:1, ESV).

Homework

Jesus unconditionally loves us—the only love God can give us. Know this and say to yourself, "Someone loves me even if I feel others don't."

Assignment:

Tip Applied:_____Date: _____
Tip Mastered: _____Date: _____

August 17

Organization

Consider buying products in bulk and pouring ingredients into smaller containers, for items such as olive oil, vinegar, coffee, and so forth. It can help you save money.

Homework

If you plan on buying in bulk, make sure you have the storage space. If you choose to fill small decorative bottles, you can place them on the counter once filled. Instead of it looking like clutter, place it on a decorative tray and it will look like a matching set.

Assignment:

Tip Applied:_____Date: _____
Tip Mastered: _____Date: _____

August 18

Organization

What do you do with stacks of paper, reports, invoices, receipts, and other items that need to be filed?

Homework

Scan files for research and / or archiving. Software, such as Evernote, is a great tool. It has templates and other features pertaining to your home and business.

Source:
https://evernote.com/

Assignment:

Tip Applied:_____Date: _____
Tip Mastered: _____Date: _____

August 19

Organization

Electrical cords and cables can become a mess and look cluttered on the floor. Ever hear of cable management?

Homework

It isn't necessary to have a frustrating experience managing your desk cables. BlueLounge products provide an easy, quick solution to otherwise time-consuming tasks. Its durable products are perfect for preventing desktop cords, phone chargers, and headphone wires from cluttering your workspace. There are many options to choose from.

Source:
https://bluelounge.com/

Assignment:

Tip Applied:_____Date: _____

Tip Mastered: _____Date: _____

August 20

Organization & Charity

It is a good idea to shop for clothes before school starts. Take inventory of what each child will need. Bring them to the store to try on clothes.

Homework

Make a point of finding smaller sizes to donate from each closet. That will help you determine how much clothing to buy. Make drawers more organized by placing plastic shoeboxes in them. Consider donating, consigning, or handing down clothes that are too small.

Assignment:

Tip Applied:_____Date: _____
Tip Mastered: _____Date: _____

August 21

Organization

Purses can be so disorganized, especially when looking for an item. It's embarrassing to dig through your purse while standing in line.

Homework

Many new purses come with compartments. Use them to categorize items such as beauty products, mouth spray, candy, gum, credit cards, and so forth. Place items in a wallet with slots. Avoid putting too many coins in a change purse or your purse will become too heavy. Gift cards go in a small zipper pouch. Get the picture?

Assignment:

Tip Applied:_____Date: _____
Tip Mastered: _____Date: _____

August 22

Laughter

"Smokers asked a Christian if they can still go to heaven if they smoke cigarettes. The Christian replied, 'You can still go to heaven, but you will have to go to hell first to get a light.'"

Source:
Unknown

"A farmer lived alone in the Irish countryside except for a pet dog he loved dearly. One day the dog died, and the farmer went to the parish priest, inquiring if a mass could be said for the dead pet. Father Patrick told the farmer: 'No, we can't have services for an animal in the church, but I'll tell you what, there's a new denomination down the road, and no telling what they believe in, but maybe they'll do something for the animal.' The farmer said: 'Thanks, I'll go right away. By the way, do you think $50,000 is enough to donate for such a service?' to which Father Patrick replied: 'Why didn't you tell me the dog was Catholic?'"

Source:
https://javacasa.com/humor/church.htm

August 23

Spirituality

"But they who wait for the Lord shall renew their strength; they shall mount up with wings like eagles; they shall run and not be weary; they shall walk and not faint" (Isaiah 40:31, ESV).

Homework

Eagles are the only birds that can fly above storms and rain clouds. The eagle animal is associated with ambition, duty, fortitude, and willpower. Eagles have amazing eyesight and can detect prey up to two miles away. Aspire to be like an eagle. Strive to be strong and fearless.

Assignment:

Tip Applied:_____Date: _____
Tip Mastered: _____Date: _____

August 24

Tip

Use a nylon stocking to save money. Secure it to the washer return hose. The lint will be collected, preventing your sink from becoming clogged.

Homework

Lint will accumulate in the stocking. It should be replaced in a few months or when full. If you decide to buy the washer lint catcher and / or trap from the store, that is another option.

Assignment:

Tip Applied:_____Date: _____
Tip Mastered: _____Date: _____

August 25

Charity

What can you donate to a local shelter such as a homeless and / or women's shelter?

Homework

- Pack a bag with travel-size soaps, shampoos, and other toiletries from your hotel stay
- Money
- Underwear, diapers, blankets, school supplies, first aid kit and ear buds
- Look in your closets and drawers for clothes to donate along with socks and shoes
- Donate books and magazines, too
- Ask for a receipt for a tax deduction
- It should be placed in your tax folder for the following year

Assignment:

Tip Applied:_____Date: _____
Tip Mastered: _____Date: _____

August 26

Organization

Does your partner keep a pile of dirty clothes next to the bed that they may or may not wear again before washing?

Homework

The closet should be equipped with hooks to hang clothes, which can be attached over the door. Ask them to sort the pile of clean and dirty clothes before and / or on laundry day. Without action, it won't be washed. After a while, they will get the routine. However, unless they do it, you may have to wash them anyway. You can make a compromise and have them take chores from you as you tackle the laundry. Can't say you didn't try.

Assignment:

Tip Applied:_____Date: _____
Tip Mastered: _____Date: _____

August 27

Organization

Baskets are a great tool to help keep your home organized.

Homework

Use baskets for mail, magazines, other papers, dog / cat toys, and so forth. Keep baskets near the door for pockets of change, eyeglasses, and keys. Display the baskets so they look attractive.

Assignment:

Tip Applied:_____Date: _____
Tip Mastered: _____Date: _____

August 28

Laughter

Q: How do you make holy water?
A: Get regular water and boil the devil out of it.

Q. Who was the first tennis player in the bible?
A. Joseph, because he served in Pharaoh's court.

Source:
https://christiancamppro.com/the-constantly-growing-list-of-funny-christian-jokes-with-pictures/

"A man and his ever-nagging wife went on vacation to Jerusalem. While they were there, the wife passed away. The undertaker told the husband, 'You can have her shipped home for $5,000, or you can bury her here, in the Holy Land for $150.' The man thought about it and told him that he would have her shipped home. The undertaker asked, 'Why would you spend $5,000 to ship your wife home, when it would be wonderful to be buried here and you would only spend $150?' The man replied, "Long ago a man died here, was buried here, and 3 days later he rose from the dead. I just can't take that chance.'"

Source:
Good Times Detroit Newspaper Eastside Edition, July 23rd August 6th, 2022

August 29

Spirituality

"Therefore, let those who suffer according to God's will entrust their souls to a faithful Creator while doing good" (1 Peter 4:19, ESV).

Homework

This scripture helps describe what to do when bad things happen to good people. The test of faith is common to all of us. Never give up because God will reward and honor you in the end!

Assignment:

Tip Applied:_____Date: _____
Tip Mastered: _____Date: _____

August 30

Organization

Have your kitchen cabinets become too cluttered? How difficult is it to cram everything in?

Homework

When you handle each item, ask yourself this question, "Would I take this item with me if I were moving?" Donate old mugs, bowls, utensils, and small appliances you don't use—especially if they're outdated. When multiples of the same item are together, pick the best of the best and get rid of the rest.

Assignment:

Tip Applied:_____Date: _____
Tip Mastered: _____Date: _____

August 31

Organization & Time Management

Want to be organized like a professional organizer?

Every day pick up items in each room that do not belong there. Go in each room and place items in their "home."

Homework

If you do this every day, you will be organized like a professional organizer. Never leave a room without glancing around to see if there are several misplaced items. You will be able to find everything the first time you look for it and put it away immediately in its "home." A quick pick-up every day will be a breeze. Never accumulate clutter or it will overwhelm you. Your house will be tidy, neat, and you won't be embarrassed if someone stops by unexpectedly.

Assignment:

Tip Applied:_____Date: _____
Tip Mastered: _____Date: _____

Chapter 9

September

An excellent wife, who can find her?
For her worth is far above jewels.
The heart of her husband trusts in her,
And he will have no lack of gain.
She does him good and not evil
All the days of her life.
She looks for wool and linen,
And works with her hands in delight.
She is like merchant ships;
She brings her food from afar.
And she rises while it is still night
And gives food to her household,
And portions to her attendants.
She considers a field and buys it;
From her earnings she plants a vineyard.
She surrounds her waist with strength
And makes her arms strong.
She senses that her profit is good;
Her lamp does not go out at night.
She stretches out her hands to the distaff,

And her hands grasp the spindle.
She extends her hand to the poor,
And she stretches out her hands to the needy.
She is not afraid of the snow for her household,
For all her household are clothed with scarlet.
She makes coverings for herself;
Her clothing is fine linen and purple.
Her husband is known in the gates,
When he sits among the elders of the land.
She makes linen garments and sells them,
And supplies belts to the tradesmen.
Strength and dignity are her clothing,
And she smiles at the future.
She opens her mouth in wisdom,
And the teaching of kindness is on her tongue.
She watches over the activities of her household,
And does not eat the bread of idleness.
Her children rise up and bless her;
Her husband also, and he praises her, saying:
"Many daughters have done nobly,
But you excel them all."
Charm is deceitful and beauty is vain,
But a woman who fears the LORD, she shall be praised.
Give her the product of her hands,
And let her works praise her in the gates. (Proverbs 31:10-31, NASB)

September 1

Time Management

Do you talk on the phone but need to get your chores done?

Homework

You can wipe down a bathroom, fold a load of laundry, dust, or wash dishes while talking on the phone. Multitasking is a plus! Today earbuds are available, so you have hands free.

Assignment:

Tip Applied:_____Date: _____

Tip Mastered: _____Date: _____

September 2

Organization

Mottos for the whole family.

Homework

- If you take it out, put it back
- If you open it, close it
- If you see it on the floor, pick it up
- If you move it, put it back
- If you make a mess, clean it up
- If you eat out of it, wash it
- If you empty it, fill it up
- If you wear it, hang it up or put it in the laundry

Assignment:

Tip Applied:_____Date: _____
Tip Mastered: _____Date: _____

September 3

Organization

Are your children throwing their clothes on the floor?

Homework

- Place a basketball hoop over a laundry basket or hamper. Make it fun for them.
- Teach them to hang up their clothes and stand on a stool if they can't reach.
- Put clean clothes in the drawers if they are older.
- If they don't do it, then they are restricted from playing outside, toys, computer electronics, and / or TV.

Assignment:

Tip Applied:_____Date: _____
Tip Mastered: _____Date: _____

September 4

Organization

To save space in the closets, remove empty hangers when you take the garment off. Hangers take up a lot of space, especially if the clothes rack is stuffed.

Homework

Empty the hangers into a separate laundry basket. All your hangers will be available when you wash the laundry so you can hang up the damp and dry clothes. Putting away the hanging laundry takes a little more time, but it is worth it! There will be more room in your closet to see your clothes when getting dressed.

Assignment:

Tip Applied:_____Date: _____
Tip Mastered: _____Date: _____

September 5

Time Management & Organization

Are you a really organized person already? Especially in your closet?

Homework:

Take a look at your closet full of clothes, and decide what you don't want to wear anymore.

- Separate all sleeveless tops and blouses and place them categorized on the rack. Now put color in order, starting with light colors and ending with darker shades. You will be able to see how many of the same items that you didn't know you had.
- Next, short sleeve, long sleeve, and sweaters.
- Capris, casual pants, jeans, etc.
- Skirts and dresses the same way as above.
- For men the same method but adding dress shirts, slacks, vests, suits, suit jackets, long sleeve light zippered sweaters, sweatshirts, and hoodies.

When you need to pick out an outfit, you can match the outfit according to the weather, color, and occasion.

Assignment:

Tip Applied:_____Date: _____
Tip Mastered: _____Date: _____

September 6

Etiquette

Avoid using a speakerphone during a telephone call in a vehicle with others present.

Homework

Tell the caller that others can hear the conversation. You can ask whether they want to continue the call or not. If others are present and something is said about someone in the vehicle, it can be embarrassing to the caller.

Assignment:

Tip Applied:_____Date: _____
Tip Mastered: _____Date: _____

September 7

Organization

It's time to shop for additional school supplies once you receive this year's supply list from school.

Homework

Shop for school supplies when items are on sale. Label children's names on their supplies. Use organizers and binders for their desks. Backpacks can get crammed, so use zipper pouches for categorized items. Most office supply stores have a giant sale in July and August. They are very inexpensive, so pick up a few extras.

Assignment:

Tip Applied:_____Date: _____
Tip Mastered: _____Date: _____

September 8

Spirituality

"Therefore, confess your sins to one another, and pray for one another so that you may be healed. A prayer of a righteous person, when it is brought about, can accomplish much" (James 5:16, NASB).

Homework

When you're very sick, ask a friend, minister and / or deacon to pray for you and to anoint you with oil. Ask your church to place your name on a prayer chain. Have faith that you will be healed!

Assignment:

Tip Applied:_____Date: _____
Tip Mastered: _____Date: _____

September 9

Laughter

"Attending a wedding for the first time, a little girl whispered to her mother, 'Why is the bride dressed in white?' 'Because white is the color of happiness, and today is the happiest day of her life.' The child thought about this for a moment, then said, 'So why is the groom wearing black?'"

Source:
https://javacasa.com/humor/mouthsofbabes.htm

"A woman called a church and asked to speak to the Head Hog of the Trough. The secretary said, I'm sorry, but we don't refer to our pastor as a hog." The lady said, 'I was calling to give your church ten thousand dollars.' The secretary then said, 'Well hold the phone, I think I see that fat pig coming down the hall right now.'"

Source:
https://www.javacasa.com/humor/seasonal.htm

September 10

Organization

Wonderful products exist to repair the hems on ripped slacks, skirts, dress shirts, T-shirts, and so forth.

Homework

In a quick emergency, use a strip of double-sided tape. Also, fabric glue will not dissolve when laundered or show on the garment.

Source:
https://www.joann.com/search?q=fabric%20glue&prefn1=product
Group&prefv1=Product

Assignment:

Tip Applied:_____Date: _____
Tip Mastered: _____Date: _____

September 11

Time Management

When school starts, set an early bedtime, schedule chores, and homework. Maintain a consistent bedtime schedule.

Homework

Choose clothing for small children the night before. You can prepare lunch the night before and / or in the morning. Children's chores should not conflict with their schoolwork. Having a work-life balance will make it easier for them to balance everything. One suggestion is to put the children to bed fifteen to thirty minutes before the lights go out and have them read a book. That will make them sleepy, and they will learn something from the book.

Assignment:

Tip Applied:_____Date: _____
Tip Mastered: _____Date: _____

September 12

Organization

Do you wash clothes every day because of having a large family?

Homework

Wash a load of laundry for each bedroom, so the laundry is already sorted when it comes out of the dryer. Immediately fold to prevent wrinkles and put away the clothes. Damp shirts, blouses, and slacks that come out of the dryer should be hung up immediately, so they don't need ironing.

Assignment:

Tip Applied:_____Date: _____
Tip Mastered: _____Date: _____

September 13

Charity

Do you have a musical instrument lying around that isn't being played or used anymore?

Homework

A school, student, or someone in need can benefit from the donation of the instrument. Many students from single parent families usually do not have the money to buy or rent their instrument. Otherwise, there are several places to sell it, including eBay and / or Facebook Marketplace.

Assignment:

Tip Applied:_____Date: _____
Tip Mastered: _____Date: _____

September 14

Time Management

Does your family get anxious when getting ready for school? Can you only find one shoe when leaving the house? Does everyone search under beds and around the house for missing items?

Homework

Consider putting hooks near the door where backpacks can be hung. To keep everything in one place, put shoes and coats next to the backpack. Double-check that all necessary items are on hand the night before. Having a checklist displayed helps keep everything organized.

Assignment:

Tip Applied:_____Date: _____
Tip Mastered: _____Date: _____

September 15

Organization

Do you know what happens when you organize a closet, room, or area that is stuffed to the maximum?

Homework

Breathing will be easier for you. There is more to clutter than just that! Clutter takes up space and stagnates the environment. In some cases, people have developed breathing problems such as asthma from clutter.

I experienced it when I stayed at my relative's house. Her closet in the bedroom was stuffed to the brim. The next day, we decluttered it and donated most of it. The closet was nearly empty. I was able to breathe better that night and could not believe the difference it had made. It is really true that clutter can harm the environment you're living in.

Assignment:

Tip Applied:_____Date: _____
Tip Mastered: _____Date: _____

September 16

Laughter

"Saint Peter greets Bill Gates at the pearly gates and says, 'Bill, have you got a million dollars to get into heaven?' Bill Gates says, 'No, I have a billion dollars, and don't you know, these gates are named after me!'"

"A man went on a vacation to Florida from their home in Alaska. He waited for his wife to come the next day to stay with him. He tried to e-mail her but could not remember it. He messed up, and instead his e-mail was sent to a preacher's wife whose husband died the day before. The message said: 'Having fun, but it sure is hot down here. I can't wait for your arrival here soon.'"

Source:
https://javacasa.com/humor/pearlygate.htm

September 17

Spirituality

"'For I know the plans that I have for you,' declares the Lord, 'plans for prosperity and not for disaster, to give you a future and a hope'" (Jeremiah 29:11, NASB).

Homework

This is such an encouraging verse. Say it over and over until it gets into your spirit. God leads us to the Lord and guides us to where He wants us to go as long as we obey Him. When we are going through a trial and can't see the light at the end of the tunnel, know that He has plans and a future for you.

Assignment:

Tip Applied:_____Date: _____
Tip Mastered: _____Date: _____

September 18

Time Management

Find a quick way to tape quantities of boxes when moving or shipping.

Homework

The Duck BladeSafe Tape Gun Dispenser has a retractable blade and will save you from accidental cuts. Taping a box is a breeze and it goes fast. It will not peel off! You can buy this product online and it's also sold in stores.

Source:
https://www.findtape.com/Duck-BladeSafe-Tape-Dispenser/p638/?idx=0&tid=0

Assignment:

Tip Applied:_____Date: _____
Tip Mastered: _____Date: _____

September 19

Organization

Make a pleasant environment by organizing your home office.

Homework

Organize small office supplies inside drawers by using an inside desk organizer. Use a stand-up file holder with attractive labeled folders where you can clearly see the labels. A lamp, calendar, and possibly a plant, candles, and decorative accessories will be added to the décor. Always have office supplies on hand. It is easier to think, find things, make decisions, and have a vision in an organized office.

Assignment:

Tip Applied:_____Date: _____
Tip Mastered: _____Date: _____

September 20

Organization

Are you a procrastinator?

A person who habitually puts off doing things; delay, procrastinate, lag, loiter, dawdle, dally; move or act slowly so as to fall behind; usually implies putting something off.

Homework

When you ask someone in your house to put things away, do they respond, "I'll do it in a minute?" When you ask a question again do they say, "Oh, I forgot; I'll get to it soon?" Finally, when you ask a question a third time do they say, "You're nagging me?"

You can't win, so do it yourself, hire someone, or have a serious discussion with your housemate or children. Give them choices. Don't feel alone, it happens to a lot of families.

Source:
https://www.merriam-webster.com/dictionary/procrastinator

Assignment:

Tip Applied:_____Date: _____
Tip Mastered: _____Date: _____

September 21

Time Management

How hectic is your morning routine? As you prepare to go to work, school, or just to begin the day, do you need to find toiletries?

Homework

In the medicine cabinet, arrange grooming products in the order in which you use them. For makeup, women can use a variety of cosmetic bags. Store your cosmetic brushes in a cup for easy viewing. Use compartments to organize items in a drawer. As you use them, take them out and put them away.

Assignment:

Tip Applied:_____Date: _____
Tip Mastered: _____Date: _____

September 22

Laughter

During our mission trip to Dearborn, Michigan, one of our missionaries ministering to Muslim women had a tooth infection. She was picked up by my husband for a dentist appointment. While the women were learning English, he went through the classroom with my eight-year-old granddaughter where all the Muslim women were dressed in black burkas and hijabs. My granddaughter remarked, "They are the most beautiful brides I have ever seen."

Source:
Ava J. Kallmes

# September 23

Spirituality

"A joyful heart is good medicine, but a broken spirit dries up the bones" (Proverbs 17:22, NASB).

Homework

Instead of getting caught up in the negatives, find joy in every situation. If you disagree with another person, don't quench their spirit and / or agree to disagree. Thank Jesus anyway because that is what he wants from us. Be thankful; you will become blessed.

Assignment:

Tip Applied:_____Date: _____
Tip Mastered: _____Date: _____

September 24

Organization

Have you ever wondered what to do with all the vases accumulated from people who sent you flowers?

Homework

Bring one to a florist who can fill it with flowers and bring it to someone in the hospital, friend, or a neighbor. Take several vases to a consignment store. Keep only a few pieces that you like to avoid clutter. Furthermore, extra vases might not fit in your cupboard.

Assignment:

Tip Applied:_____Date: _____
Tip Mastered: _____Date: _____

September 25

Organization

Photographs are incredibly valuable today, especially old ones. Keeping them in an acid-free box or storing them with acid-free paper is the best storage method.

Homework

The photographs should be free of paper clips, rubber bands, glue, or tape. A plastic page, box, or adhesive that isn't acid-free can release potentially harmful vapors that damage photos permanently. The negatives in the photo envelopes can be thrown away because you no longer need them. If you want, you can scan the photos instead.

Assignment:

Tip Applied:_____Date: _____

Tip Mastered: _____Date: _____

September 26

Organization

Are you a visual person who needs to see a reminder written in a post-it note?

Homework

Consider writing yourself a note. As a reminder, put post-it notes in your vehicle and stick them where you see them. So that you don't forget them, you can place them on a mirror, keys, purse, or refrigerator and so forth.

Assignment:

Tip Applied:_____Date: _____
Tip Mastered: _____Date: _____

September 27

Tip

Q. What is the opposite effect of laughter?
A. Crying

Homework

We know women cry and guys rarely do. On average, women weep forty-seven times a year, but guys bawl just seven times. Did you know emotional crying lowers stress, produces endorphins that can decrease pain, and rids the body of various toxins?

Sources:
https://www.amazon.com/Choose-Better-Path-Overcoming-Parents/dp/0998040509

"Choose A Better Path," by Kent Darcie, pp. 16-17.

Assignment:

Tip Applied:_____Date: _____
Tip Mastered: _____Date: _____

September 28

Spirituality

"But the one who endures to the end will be saved" (Matthew 24:13, NASB).

Homework

What does it mean to be saved? Ask Jesus into your heart and the Holy Spirit will come in. That hole in your soul will be filled and you will not feel empty ever again!

Assignment:

Tip Applied:_____Date: _____
Tip Mastered: _____Date: _____

September 29

Organization

The definition of a professional organizer:

A professional organizer is an experienced person who uses their talent and skills to declutter and reorganize spaces, rooms, homes, and / or offices, and so forth, creating order out of chaos and clutter. The goal is an environment that offers peace and streamlines their quality of life.

What is a good benefit of Obsessive Compulsive Disorder (OCD)?

They are very strong on organization. Possibly the most recognizable form of OCD, this type involves obsessions about things being in precisely the right place or symmetrical.

What is an inadequate OCD?

Accumulating and saving an excessive number of items, gradual buildup of clutter in living spaces, and difficulty discarding things are usually the first signs and symptoms of a hoarding disorder, which often surfaces during the teenage to early adult years.

Homework

How I became a professional organizer is a question I get asked often. Visioning the proper placement of items is a gift. It is called (OCD), Obsessive Compulsive Disorder. On a scale from left to right, Martha Stewart is (strong to perfection) all the way to the left, and a hoarder is (inadequate) all the way to the right. Professional organizers are closer to Stewart in terms of skill level and vision. The hoarder may need medication and a therapist to help them climb out of their enormous clutter.

Most people are in the middle of the scale and are capable of becoming more organized with some training.

Sources:
https://www.mayoclinic.org/diseases-conditions/hoarding-disorder/symptoms-causes/syc-20356056#:

https://www.mayoclinic.org/diseases-conditions/obsessive-compulsive-disorder/symptoms-causes/syc-20354432

Assignment:

Tip Applied:_____Date: _____
Tip Mastered: _____Date: _____

September 30

Tip

Your body can benefit from essential oils. Hundreds of plants, flowers, trees, and herbs produce essential oils. These oils have different purposes for the body and mind.

Homework

The essential oils can be placed in a diffuser next to your bed and / or family room so that everyone can benefit from them. Apply oil to the bottom of your feet before going to bed and it will work all night long. Use the type of oil for your ailment.

Assignment:

Tip Applied:_____Date: _____

Tip Mastered: _____Date: _____

Chapter 10

October

And He was saying to them all, "If anyone wants to come after Me, he must deny himself, take up his cross daily, and follow Me (Luke 9:23, NASB).

October 1

Laughter

Q. Do you know why Moses and his people were wandering in the desert for forty years?

A. Because even back then, the men would not stop and ask for directions.

Source:
Debbie Tebbe

While watching "Mr. Rogers" with my three-year-old daughter Hannah one afternoon, I explained to her that Mr. Rogers went to live in Heaven. Hannah immediately said, "No Mama, he lives in the neighborhood!"

Source:
https://www.javacasa.com/humor/reallife.htm

October 2

Organization

Many consumers complain about their washer smelling like mold after washing clothes. What should I do?

Homework

Keep the lid and / or door open overnight after you have finished washing. The washer will stop smelling the next morning. Additionally, Affresh tablets can be placed in the washing machine every few months to clean out the washer. Be especially aware of front-loading machines. The large rubber outer seal (gasket) around the door is where mold and gunk collect. Wipe clean periodically.

Assignment:

Tip Applied:_____Date: _____
Tip Mastered: _____Date: _____

October 3

Organization

What can you do with a cluttered refrigerator?

Homework

Organize your shelves by purchasing clear bins that are easy to label and place them on shelves. They can be used for breads, condiments, sauces, yogurt, beverages, and so forth. I admit that it is sometimes difficult to get family members to return items back to their "home."

Assignment:

Tip Applied:_____Date: _____
Tip Mastered: _____Date: _____

October 4

Tip

October is National Breast Cancer awareness month.

Homework

Did you forget or put off your mammogram? This is an important X-ray test for women because you may not know if you have breast cancer. Breast cancer death rates declined forty percent from 1989 to 2016 among women. The progress is attributed to improvements in early detection. Please get screened.

Source:
https://www.nationalbreastcancer.org/

Assignment:

Tip Applied:_____Date: _____
Tip Mastered: _____Date: _____

October 5

Laughter

"A Sunday School teacher began her lesson with a question: 'Boys and girls, what do we know about God?' A hand shot up in the air. 'He is an artist!' said the kindergarten boy. 'Really?! How do you know?' the teacher asked. 'You know, "Our Father, who does art in Heaven"?'

"A four-year-old boy prayed this prayer: 'And forgive us our trash baskets as we forgive those who put trash in our baskets. Amen.'"

Source:
https://javacasa.com/humor/mouthsofbabes.htm

October 6

Spirituality

"Therefore, I say to you, all things for which you pray and ask, believe that you have received them, and they will be granted to you" (Mark 11:24, NASB).

Homework

In the Bible, God directs us to pray and ask according to His will. If He says yes, no, or wait, we are supposed to obey. If the answer is "Yes," then go for it but make sure you stay on the straight and narrow road. "No" is also an answer and then you need to come up with a Plan B and figure out what the Lord is telling you to do. We understand that waiting is difficult, but if you want to be in His perfect will, then you must wait! Once it happens, you will realize why you waited, and it will exceed your expectations.

Assignment:

Tip Applied:_____Date: _____
Tip Mastered: _____Date: _____

October 7

Organization

Each week, children bring home artwork, graded tests, projects, homework, awards, and assignments. How does one deal with all of that?

Homework

You can display it on the refrigerator, kitchen cabinets, or closet doors for one week, then remove it. Don't be a fan of posting on cabinets or doors. Put up a cork bulletin board so it looks tidy. Throw away anything that is not important. Memorabilia boxes can be used to store awards and precious artwork. Don't overdo it!

Assignment:

Tip Applied:_____Date: _____
Tip Mastered: _____Date: _____

October 8

Tip

Whenever you enter a public restroom, use the end stall. These stalls are used less frequently and should be cleaner.

Homework:

Be sure to cover the toilet seat with toilet paper or a seat cover. Before leaving the restroom, wash your hands and don't touch the door. Instead, push it open with your elbow or with your baby finger. Then you'll be germ-free!

Sometimes I ask my husband if he uses the seat covers provided. "Oh, you mean doilies for the seats?" "No, they are too girly."

Assignment:

Tip Applied:_____Date: _____
Tip Mastered: _____Date: _____

October 9

Tip

Brush, floss, and / or Waterpik your teeth to keep tarter and plaque from leading to gum disease.

Homework

It is recommended to brush and floss daily and / or use a Waterpik. You may find it helpful to use a Waterpik with mouthwash added if you suffer from gum disease, such as gingivitis or pyorrhea. It's up to fifty percent more effective for improving gum health compared to using string floss.

Source:
https://www.waterpik.com/

Assignment:

Tip Applied:_____Date: _____
Tip Mastered: _____Date: _____

October 10

Tip

Today is National Crime Prevention Month. What are you going to do about it?

Homework

- Always lock your homes and vehicles when you enter and exit the door. You can never be too safe.
- Install a home alarm system to sleep peacefully at night.
- When you are away, set timers for the lights.
- If you sense danger in a parking lot, hold your pepper spray or car keys pointing towards them, just in case.
- Invest in a video doorbell camera.
- Consider organizing a Neighborhood Watch Program.

Source:
https://www.ncpc.org/

Assignment:

Tip Applied:_____Date: _____
Tip Mastered: _____Date: _____

October 11

Laughter

"An elderly woman had just returned to her home from an evening of church services when she was startled by an intruder. She caught the man in the act of robbing her home of its valuables and yelled, 'Stop! Acts 2:38!'

The burglar stopped in his tracks. The woman calmly called the police and explained what she had done. As the officer cuffed the man to take him in, he asked the burglar, 'Why did you just stand there? All the old lady did was yell a scripture to you.' 'Scripture?' replied the burglar. 'She said she had an ax and two 38's!'"

Source:
https://www.javacasa.com/humor/sermon.htm

October 12

Spirituality

"I have loved you with an everlasting love; therefore, I have continued my faithfulness to you" (Jeremiah 31:3, ESV).

Homework

The Bible is God's love letter to us. The words are so sweet and full of joy. Jesus is our best friend, and He will always be at your side. He loved us before the beginning of time and throughout eternity.

Assignment:

Tip Applied:_____Date: _____
Tip Mastered: _____Date: _____

October 13

Tip

Do you know the number of minutes it takes for germs to die on a surface cleaned with a disinfecting wipe?

Homework

Sanitizing wipes leave behind a bacteria-killing disinfectant. Don't touch the surface until three minutes are up. Sanitizing wipes are effective for the coronavirus, flu, and other infections.

For both Lysol and Clorox Disinfecting Wipes, the hard surface must remain wet for at least four minutes—ten minutes is best—for germs and bacteria to be killed.

Source:
https://www.thespruce.com/definition-disinfecting-sanitizing-cleaning-4799721

Assignment:

Tip Applied:_____Date: _____
Tip Mastered: _____Date: _____

October 14

Tip

Disasters happen all the time around the world, such as earthquakes, hurricanes, tornados, floods, fires—including the coronavirus pandemic.

Homework

Are you prepared for an emergency? What if you had to leave your home?

Three websites for general disaster preparedness are:

- Being ready for disasters takes preparation, not luck. Know your risk, make a plan, build a kit with the link directions.

Source:
https://www.ready.gov/

- Get training, certification, give blood, and many more services.

Source:
https://www.redcross.org/

- Find information on disasters and assistance, floods, emergencies, and so forth.

Source:
https://www.fema.gov/

Assignment:

Tip Applied:_____Date: _____
Tip Mastered: _____Date: _____

October 15

Time Management

Do you know how many gallons of water the average dishwasher uses to clean and wash one load of dishes?

Homework

Energy-efficient dishwashers use approximately four gallons of water per load to wash and sanitize dishes. Washing the same load by hand would require four times as much water, or sixteen gallons. Rinse dishes without running the water continuously. Practice water conservation. Several regions of the country are suffering from drought.

Assignment:

Tip Applied:_____Date: _____
Tip Mastered: _____Date: _____

October 16

Organization & Time Management

Canisters are useful for storing soaps, pods, fabric softener, and so forth for the laundry.

Homework

You will save time and be more organized with the canisters. Simply grab what you need, drop and / or pour. In addition, the bulk items that you store after filling up the canisters, need to be purchased when running low.

Assignment:

Tip Applied:_____Date: _____
Tip Mastered: _____Date: _____

October 17

Organization

Do you have too many scarves? It's hard to sift through a pile of scarves bunched in a drawer. What is the best way to organize them?

Homework

Use scarf hangers with holes for each scarf, organize by color, seasons, and type of scarf. These hooks have a small hanger at the top, so they loop over the closet bar. The hook is large to slip several scarves on one. They can also be used to store belts, ties, and other accessories. There are many types to choose from and they are inexpensive. They do not take up much space, but you may need several hangers if you have many scarves.

Assignment:

Tip Applied:_____Date: _____
Tip Mastered: _____Date: _____

October 18

Organization

Helpful tips to stage a home to sell.

Homework

- Take down all personal pictures and knickknacks.
- Put some of your furniture in storage to make the rooms look larger.
- Sell some of your furniture and furnishings that you don't want in your new home.
- Declutter each room to look like a model home.
- As hard as it may seem, paint the rooms in neutral colors and remove wallpaper if it was your color scheme and may not appeal to the new buyer.
- Tidy up the home before the open house.
- Close closet doors and toilet lids.
- Open the drapes or curtains and let in the light.
- Have a clean kitchen with little on the counters.
- A pleasant-smelling home will give the buyer a happy memory, especially with cookies in the oven.

Assignment:

Tip Applied:_____Date: _____
Tip Mastered: _____Date: _____

October 19

Laughter

"A young girl observed some plaques on the wall of the church building and asked her mother: 'Mom who are those people? Whose names are on the wall?'

Her mom replied, 'They are the people who died in the service.' Immediately came the retort: 'Did they die in the morning or the evening service?'"

Source:
https://www.javacasa.com/humor/church.htm

October 20

Spirituality

"I will instruct you and teach you in the way you should go; I will counsel you with my eye upon you" (Psalm 32:8, ESV).

Homework

We learn all about life from Jesus. He cares about each individual in a unique way. He is omnipresent—He is everywhere. He is also omnipotent—God can act everywhere because he is all-powerful. In His omniscience and knowledge, He has access to everything, anywhere, and knows all secrets.

October 21

Organization & Time Management

There comes a time when you need to clean out your spices and check expiration dates.

Homework

Go through each spice, check the dates, and separate baking and cooking spices. Duplicates should be poured in one bottle if there is room. Organize bottles with flakes, salts / peppers, meat seasoning, most used together, and so forth. Use round spinning trays or tier steps so you can find what you need faster. Baking spices go in a separate bin. When you decide to bake, pull out that container, place it on the counter, and everything will be in one place. You don't need to go through all the other spices to bake.

Assignment:

Tip Applied:_____Date: _____
Tip Mastered: _____Date: _____

October 22

Organization & Time Management

Light bulbs need a home to live in too, so their replacements can be found quickly when a bulb burns out.

Homework

Organize all the bulbs in a plastic container, basket, or bin. The bulbs will be easy to find. Be sure that you have the right type of bulb and the correct wattage for every outlet in the house. The cost of LED lights is a little more expensive, but they are energy-efficient, saving a lot on electricity, and will last years longer.

Assignment:

Tip Applied:_____Date: _____
Tip Mastered: _____Date: _____

October 23

Time Management

Did you forget your lunch, paperwork, and / or anything else before leaving home?

Homework

Place your keys or purse or the items you will need before leaving. If that doesn't work for you, place the items in your vehicle the night before. You can put a post-it-note on your keys as a reminder.

Assignment:

Tip Applied:_____Date: _____
Tip Mastered: _____Date: _____

October 24

Organization & Time Management

Are you searching through all your keys before finding the one you need to open your vehicle, home, or other doors?

Homework

The number of different key designs has reached over seven hundred. There are a lot of interesting key blanks to choose from. They are powder coated so the design won't wear off. Under the design is a brass key. These are great for organizing keys by color and design! There are keys that are marked with a name, such as "Home," and you can find it immediately. Locksmiths and hardware shops can cut these keys for you.

Source:
https://keysrcool.com/

Assignment:

Tip Applied:_____Date: _____
Tip Mastered: _____Date: _____

October 25

Organization

Your individual photos can be organized into categories by family, vacations, birthdays, weddings, and so forth. Discard any images of obscure landscaping, blurry scenes, or unrecognizable faces.

Homework

You can throw away the envelopes and negatives. Photographs should be placed in acid-free boxes until they can be placed in an album or scrapbook.

Try this if you would like a simpler way to view photos. In a typical photo storage box, there are ten 4x6 colored boxes inside to categorize photos. Each box can be labeled and categorized by events or people.

Source:
https://www.michaels.com/search?q=photo%20organizers

Assignment:

Tip Applied:_____Date: _____
Tip Mastered: _____Date: _____

October 26

Laughter

"Bill Gates arrives at the pearly gates. 'Well, Bill,' said God, I'm not sure whether to send you to Heaven or Hell. You helped society by putting a computer in almost every home in the world. I'm going to let you decide where you want to go.' God said, 'You can take a peek at both places briefly if it will help you decide.

'Shall we look at Hell first?' Bill was amazed! He saw a white sandy beach with clear waters. There were thousands of beautiful men and women playing in the water and laughing. The sun was shining, and the temperature was perfect. 'If this is Hell, I can't wait to see heaven.'

So off they went to Heaven. Bill saw puffy white clouds, blue sky with angels playing harps and singing. It was nice, but surely not as enticing as Hell. 'God, I do believe I would like to go to Hell.' 'As you desire,' said God.

Two weeks later, God decided to check up on the late billionaire to see how things were going. He found Bill shackled to a wall, screaming amongst the hot flames in a dark cave. He was being burned and tortured by demons. 'How you doing, Bill?' asked God. Bill responded with anguish and despair, 'This is awful! This is not what I expected at all! What happened to the beach and the beautiful women playing in the water?' 'Oh THAT!' said God. 'That was the Screensaver.'"

Source:
https://www.pleacher.com/chumor/humor/billgate.html

330

October 27

Spirituality

"Take hold of instruction; do not let go. Guard her, for she is your life" (Proverbs 4:13, NASB).

Homework

This scripture refers to instructions from a father to his son. In the Bible, you find instructions for life. We use the Bible as our textbook for what to do, when to do it, and how to do it. Get to know your Bible! After you've read it, there is just something that happens to you spiritually.

Assignment:

Tip Applied:_____Date: _____
Tip Mastered: _____Date: _____

October 28

Organization

Coupons are an excellent way to save money. But many people forget to bring them along when they go shopping.

Homework

Place them in a clear plastic file folder and label each category as follows:

- Grocery
- Restaurants
- Department stores
- Bed Bath & Beyond, (they take expired coupons)
- Specialty stores

Keep them in your vehicle to always have them with you when you are shopping. Every month check the folder for expired coupons. Place new coupons every week or two inside the folder. Put the money in your pocket instead of theirs.

My husband was going to Bed Bath & Beyond. I gave him the folder of coupons to use for his purchases. When he came home, I asked him if he used them. He said they were all expired. I sighed and told him they took expired coupons.

Assignment:

Tip Applied:_____Date: _____
Tip Mastered: _____Date: _____

October 29

Time Management & Organization

How many emails do you receive every day? Do you have a hard time keeping track and finding them when needed?

Homework

Sort your emails into folders on the left side of your email window like a filing cabinet. Use action folders to help prioritize your emails, so they don't fall through the cracks. It will be much easier to locate emails when needed. If you are a visual person, you can print them as a "to do" reminder. Delete when completed or if they are not important. Clean out spam and trash folders weekly.

Assignment:

Tip Applied:_____Date: _____
Tip Mastered: _____Date: _____

October 30

Etiquette

Keep antibacterial wipes, hand sanitizer, on your person, in your vehicle, purse, or at your desk for places where you cannot wash your hands before and after eating.

Homework

When getting ready for a meal in a restaurant, use a wipe or hand sanitizer every time to kill any germs and bacteria. Set it on the table so others will use it too.

Assignment:

Tip Applied:_____Date: _____
Tip Mastered: _____Date: _____

October 31

Organization & Charity

How do you handle all the Halloween candy?

Homework

As you pile it, sort it by candy bars, gum, hard candies, chips, money, and boxes of sweets. Donate what you have left over to a Sunday school, club, work, or public school.

Assignment:

Tip Applied:_____Date: _____
Tip Mastered: _____Date: _____

Chapter 11

November

"Come now, and let us debate your case,"
Says the LORD,
Though your sins are as scarlet,
They shall become as white as snow;
Though they are red like crimson,
They shall be like wool. (Isaiah 1:18, NASB)

November 1

Organization

Organize crafts by categories, such as knitting, beading, scrapbooking, painting, woodworking, kits, and so forth.

Homework

For specific crafts, invest in storage containers. This will make it easier to find, work on, and store them for different projects. There are so many different types of containers for each craft! Find the best ones that suit your needs.

Assignment:

Tip Applied:_____Date: _____
Tip Mastered: _____Date: _____

November 2

Time Management

You're hosting Thanksgiving and don't know what to do first?

Homework

There is a "Thanksgiving checklist" you can google on the internet that outlines what you should be doing each day and week leading up to the big day. This can help with time management and minimize stress.

Source:
https://www.suburbansimplicity.com/thanksgiving-planner-printable-checklist/

Assignment:

Tip Applied:_____Date: _____
Tip Mastered: _____Date: _____

November 3

Tip

Is it necessary to have a password to log in and lock your cellphone?

Homework

Yes, this is your first line of defense against people looking at your emails, photos, passwords, and credit card history. The thief will have a difficult time cracking the code and stealing your personal information. Do you lock your doors? This is also true of your cellphone.

Assignment:

Tip Applied:_____Date: _____
Tip Mastered: _____Date: _____

November 4

Laughter

"Since many families were unable to send their children to school because of the Covid-19 pandemic, they had to homeschool. In a FaceTime conversation, a TV celebrity asked a famous comedian, 'How is it going with homeschooling your elementary kids?' The comedian said, 'Kids, it's recess time, I need a drink!'"

Source:
TV blooper

"In the middle of the children's sermon, I was telling the preschoolers that God makes trees and water and apples and cherries. God makes everything. Immediately one little boy complained, 'God doesn't make my bed!'"

Source:
https://www.javacasa.com/humor/mouthsofbabes.htm

November 5

Spirituality

"The Lord is not slow about His promise, as some count slowness, but is patient toward you, not willing for any to perish, but for all to come to repentance" (2 Peter 3:9, NASB).

Homework

Whenever the Lord makes a promise, He will never break it. The Lord does not want anyone to perish without salvation, so that you may dwell with Him for eternity. Please repent now before it is too late!

Assignment:

Tip Applied:_____Date: _____
Tip Mastered: _____Date: _____

November 6

Organization

Make sure a room is clutter-free before you leave it.

Homework

Check to see if anything is misplaced. If so, pick it up and put it back in its "home." Ensure that items from different rooms are placed in the correct rooms. Go back and put the items where they belong if there are several of them. Every member of the household needs to follow this rule.

Assignment:

Tip Applied:_____Date: _____
Tip Mastered: _____Date: _____

November 7

Time Management

Make sure to clean up as you cook.

Homework

Rather than filling the sink with dishes, rinse off the food, and place them in the dishwasher while you prepare the meal. If you think that is tedious, place the dishes in the sink and while the food is cooking, rinse and put them in the dishwasher. Otherwise, rinse dishes and place in the dishwasher after everyone eats. Teach family members to place dishes in the sink to save you time and learn responsibility.

Assignment:

Tip Applied:_____Date: _____
Tip Mastered: _____Date: _____

November 8

Time Management

Spills should be wiped up immediately.

Homework

Whether it's a splash of tomato sauce on the stove or makeup on the bathroom counter, it's easier to remove it when you wipe it right away. Disinfecting wipes are quick and sanitizing to use as needed.

Assignment:

Tip Applied:_____Date: _____
Tip Mastered: _____Date: _____

November 9

Organization

November has arrived—have you begun the daily habit of making your bed?

Homework

Making a bed only takes two minutes along with adding throw pillows. This makes the bedroom look neater. Congratulations on starting this habit. I am proud of you as well.

Assignment:

Tip Applied:_____Date: _____
Tip Mastered: _____Date: _____

November 10

Organization

It is a good idea to open every piece of mail because you never know what might be inside the envelope.

Homework

There are some people who don't open all their mail. One day, you may receive a check with hundreds to thousands of dollars when you thought it was simply junk mail. Personally, I've experienced this with clients.

Assignment:

Tip Applied:_____Date: _____
Tip Mastered: _____Date: _____

November 11

Organization

Is your desk cluttered with piles of mail, projects, and to-do folders?

Homework

Don't leave anything on your desk except what you're working on right now. Establish a current filing system in either a desk file drawer or vertical file holder on the desk and store the rest. Sort and file as you go to avoid getting overwhelmed. The documents will be easy to locate.

Assignment:

Tip Applied:_____Date: _____
Tip Mastered: _____Date: _____

November 12

Tip

Do I need to wash my fruits and vegetables before cooking and / or eating them? Yes and no, boiling water or baking in an oven will kill any bacteria. You must, however, be cautious.

Homework

Studies found that when you place produce on a cutting board or countertop, bacteria such as E. coli and listeria on your food can land there and cause contamination on the surface. Prep vegetables and fruits by thoroughly rinsing them and using a vegetable wash.

Be especially careful when cutting raw chicken on a cutting board with a knife, don't use it on anything else. Place them in the sink to be washed. Wash your hands, wipe the counter, and get a clean cutting board and knife to continue prepping. Otherwise, this can cause Salmonella which can make you become very ill and / or it can be fatal.

Source:
https://www.medicalnewstoday.com/articles/327028#contamination

Assignment:

Tip Applied:_____Date: _____
Tip Mastered: _____Date: _____

November 13

Laughter

A mother was nursing her newborn baby. Her seven-year-old son asked, "Is one white milk and the other chocolate milk?"

His mother looked at him, saying, "What do you think I am, a vending machine?"

Source:
Richard Kallmes II

"Our five-year-old daughter, Cynthia, was concerned that each time we sang a certain praise chorus, that God would stand up and lose all the candy from His lap. It took us awhile, but we finally figured out she thought we were singing, 'Let God arise and His M & M's be scattered,' when we were actually singing, 'Let God arise and His enemies be scattered.'"

Source:
https://www.javacasa.com/humor/reallife.htm

November 14

Spirituality

"Or do you not know that your body is a temple of the Holy Spirit within you, whom you have from God? You are not your own, for you were bought with a price. So glorify God in your body" (I Corinthians 6:19-20, ESV).

Homework

Eat three healthy meals a day, take your vitamins, exercise, drink plenty of water, read the Bible, and say prayers each day. The most important advice is to not take drugs, smoke, and drink excessively, or have relations before getting married. These things combine to form one giant ball of sin. Our bodies are the temple of the Holy Ghost. All of our bodies are created by God and belong to Him. To be bought by a price is to love unconditionally! You can't buy unconditional love with money!

Assignment:

Tip Applied:_____Date: _____
Tip Mastered: _____Date: _____

November 15

Time Management & Organization

New, empty bags should be placed inside the bottom of a trash can.

Homework

Make sure there are about five new trash bags at the bottom of the trash cans, so when it is time to take out the garbage, you can quickly replace the bag. You will save time this way. Train other family members to do this.

Assignment:

Tip Applied:_____Date: _____
Tip Mastered: _____Date: _____

November 16

Organization

In most households, the mail station is a constant source of frustration and clutter.

Homework

Your household should have office magazine holders that you label with each member's name. Put their incoming mail, articles, magazines, and paperwork in the holders. Make sure that they open the mail every single day. Include a to-do folder located inside each holder.

Assignment:

Tip Applied:_____Date: _____
Tip Mastered: _____Date: _____

November 17

Organization & Time Management

When you answer your land line or cell phone, do you write it down in case you need to call them back? That would include a to do for the call.

Homework

It is recommended to use a spiral notepad to write down the caller, date, message, and phone number. You may need to gather information before calling them back. Keep all messages in the notepad in case you need it later on. Keep it for reference. You may use up the notepad so buy another one.

Assignment:

Tip Applied:_____Date: _____

Tip Mastered: _____Date: _____

November 18

Time Management & Etiquette

Place your order for Christmas cards or photo cards.

Homework

Once you receive the envelopes, fill them out while watching TV. That way, you can have fun while doing it. Some people type up labels and keep them on hand for any occasion. Family and friends love receiving cards. It means you are thinking of them and they will enjoy hearing from you and seeing current photos.

Assignment:

Tip Applied:_____Date: _____
Tip Mastered: _____Date: _____

Tip

Think about pet safety during the holiday season.

Homework

Pets should be kept in a separate room with soothing music while you entertain. Take them out for comfort breaks every couple of hours. It's so easy to become distracted by the party you could forget your pet.

In case your pet escapes, a collar and ID tags must be always worn. The owner or your pet might not realize that eating mistletoe or poinsettias that decorate the interior of a home could land them a trip to the ER.

Source:
https://www.pethub.com/article/pet-safety/holiday-pet-safety

Assignment:

Tip Applied:_____Date: _____
Tip Mastered: _____Date: _____

November 20

Time Management

Do not rush through the process of purchasing gifts just to get it done. Brainstorm instead!

Homework

Discuss what they need or want with another family member. You can print out and / or tear out pages with gift ideas from websites, catalogs, and magazines. The Amazon Prime program delivers free with free postage. The returns are so easy, and they also pay for postage when you mail the item back. Start a folder labeled, "Possible Gifts" and put new ideas in it throughout the year.

Assignment:

Tip Applied:_____Date: _____
Tip Mastered: _____Date: _____

November 21

Laughter

"For the first time in their lives, two Amish ladies entered a supermarket. When they entered the dairy section, they were shocked at all the different kinds of milk available. The Amish woman asked, 'Look at the almond milk containers, how do you squeeze milk from an almond?'

It's crazy that the English would buy this stuff. Can't they just milk a cow like us?'"

True Story

Source:
TV blooper

November 22

Spirituality

"Do not neglect hospitality to strangers, for by this some have entertained angels without knowing it" (Hebrews 13:2, NASB).

Homework

My bedroom has been visited by angels twice. They were as described in the Bible. Angels have also been seen to appear as people, and they may not even be aware of it, though they are working miracles at that moment! You will feel an anointing when you see an angel, but they will look like a normal person with ordinary clothes on!

Usually, they appear when you are in trouble, but you aren't sure where they came from. Hospitality has always been a significant part of society. Be open to showing hospitality to a stranger out of love for Christ without expecting anything in return. The miracle of helping an angelic stranger is full of signs and wonders.

Assignment:

Tip Applied:_____Date: _____
Tip Mastered: _____Date: _____

November 23

Time Management

Are you hosting Thanksgiving this year and don't have time to clean the house?

Homework

- Break down and hire a housekeeper. That will save you four-five hours of time and extra work.
- Run the dishwasher before guests arrive.
- Take out dishes, platters, serving bowls, and utensils.
- Fill up soap dispensers, tissue, toilet paper, and provide clean towels.
- Walk through the house to make sure everything is neat and tidy.
- Take a deep breath and rest a few minutes before guests start arriving.

Assignment:

Tip Applied:_____Date: _____
Tip Mastered: _____Date: _____

November 24

Time Management & Organization

If you're hosting Thanksgiving this year, (whatever date that falls on) start setting the table three days before the busy holiday.

Homework

Prepare place settings with napkins, china plates, and crystal glasses on the dining room table. Add fresh flowers and candles to the table to make your guests feel special. Show them the royal treatment.

If you prefer, you can use nice paper plates with a large crowd. It's okay to wash china plates in the dishwasher if you place them on the china setting. Declutter and keep cleaning as you go. You can do this!

Buffet style is appropriate if you don't have enough room on the table to place the food. Clear the counter if there is no space on the table.

Assignment:

Tip Applied:_____Date: _____
Tip Mastered: _____Date: _____

November 25

Tip

Is your budget tight and you cannot afford to spend much money on gifts?

Homework

Remember that clearance racks and sales are often located at the back of the store. Go check them out first and save money. Enclose the gift receipt with your gift. Use coupons and the internet to locate the best price at each store.

Assignment:

Tip Applied:_____Date: _____
Tip Mastered: _____Date: _____

November 26

Spirituality

"Let the word of Christ richly dwell within you, with all wisdom teaching and admonishing one another with psalms, hymns, and spiritual songs, singing with thankfulness in your hearts to God" (Colossians 3:16, NASB).

Homework

Invite everyone to say a few words about what they are grateful for at the dinner table. Through their words, you will understand their hearts, and all will be blessed.

Assignment:

Tip Applied:_____Date: _____
Tip Mastered: _____Date: _____

November 27

Laughter

"At Sunday school, the younger children were drawing pictures illustrating biblical stories. The teacher walked by and noticed one little boy was drawing an airplane! 'Oh, what Bible story are you drawing?' she asked. 'This is the Flight into Egypt,' the little boy answered. 'See, here is Mary, Joseph, and baby Jesus. And this,' he said, pointing to the front of the plane, 'is Pontius. He's the Pilot.'"

Source:
https://www.javacasa.com/humor/mouthsofbabes.htm

November 28

Organization & Time Management

When Black Friday comes along, I love it and can't wait to continue my Christmas shopping. Shopping in the stores gets you in the mood for the holidays. Christmas music is playing, and the stores are decorated in holiday cheer.

Homework

Read your Thanksgiving circulars and map out the stores and sales you are planning to shop at. Check store sale times and prioritize the stores you want to visit. Order promotional items online to save time.

Assignment:

Tip Applied:_____Date: _____
Tip Mastered: _____Date: _____

November 29

Organization

How do you keep track of all the gifts you bought for each person?

Homework

Charge all gifts to one credit card to keep track of expenses. Record which items you bought for each person along with the prices. Set a limit for each individual. If you are the type of person who spends the same amount on children and / or grandchildren, you will know if you need to buy other gifts. This way you have accurate records. Pay the credit card off when you can.

Assignment:

Tip Applied:_____Date: _____

Tip Mastered: _____Date: _____

November 30

Organization

Many people enjoy traveling during the holidays but dread packing and unpacking.

Homework

Start by washing your laundry. Select and lay out outfits, shoes, and jewelry accessories that coordinate with the clothes. Next, pack the outfits in the suitcase. Pack toiletries last after you get yourself ready to leave. Lastly, pack a plastic bag in the suitcase for dirty clothes. Upon returning home, unpack within a day or two and wash your laundry from the plastic bag. See how easy that was?

Assignment:

Tip Applied:_____Date: _____
Tip Mastered: _____Date: _____

Chapter 12

December

Everyone who believes that Jesus is the Christ has been born of God, and everyone who loves the Father loves the child born of Him (1 John 5:1, NASB).

Time Management

Don't wait until the last minute to wrap the Christmas gifts you bought.

Homework

To give a gift, put tissue paper inside gift bags. This will save you time wrapping. Of course, for children you should wrap a few gifts. Ask others to help you.

Assignment:

Tip Applied:_____Date: _____
Tip Mastered: _____Date: _____

December 2

Time Management

Multitasking when shopping is a great help. You will save time, money, and have peace of mind when you shop in bulk.

Homework

Buy gifts in bulk and on sale. Only you will know that several people received the same gift.

Assignment:

Tip Applied:_____Date: _____
Tip Mastered: _____Date: _____

December 3

Organization

Are you running out of money for gifts and holiday expenses?

Homework

Sell furniture, expensive knickknacks, clothing, or designer items. Sell at a consignment shop, on Craigslist, eBay, and / or Facebook Marketplace. This may be a hard task to do, but sacrifices are sometimes needed.

Assignment:

Tip Applied:_____Date: _____
Tip Mastered: _____Date: _____

December 4

Organization

Do you have gift cards scattered throughout the house?

Homework

Gather the cards together in one place and categorize them by stores, restaurants, and so forth. Make use of the gift cards for someone on your list. So, what are you waiting for? These will make wonderful gifts.

Assignment:

Tip Applied:_____Date: _____
Tip Mastered: _____Date: _____

December 5

Organization

Now is the time to put up the Christmas tree.

Homework

If you are going to buy a fresh tree or have an artificial tree in the attic or basement, get cracking! Organize your ornaments and check that the Christmas lights work. Have everything organized and ready to go to get started. Ask family members to help so it is not all on you.

Assignment:

Tip Applied:_____Date: _____
Tip Mastered: _____Date: _____

December 6

Spirituality

Have you ever wondered why Christians decorate their trees and homes with ornaments? Knowing the meaning will make your decoration more significant.

Homework

- The **tree** symbolizes the birth of Christ, His resurrection, and the cross He died on.
- **Lights** are symbolic of how Jesus is the light of the world.
- A **red** ornament represents the blood that He shed for our sins.
- **Purple** ornaments symbolize royalty.
- The **star** at the top reminds us of the Star of David that led the people and wise men to Jesus in the manger after the angel announced Christ's birth.

Assignment:

Tip Applied:_____Date: _____

Tip Mastered: _____Date: _____

December 7

Organization

When you receive Christmas cards in the mail, what do you do with them?

Homework

You can tape cards around windows, doors, or string them across a wall. When you are finished displaying them, place cards in a photo album or a memorabilia box. The people who sent you these took the time, money, and energy to do so, so take a moment to enjoy each card! Make sure you don't keep cards in the envelopes. It appears uncaring. After Christmas, keep cards and newsletters from immediate family or friends and recycle the rest.

Assignment:

Tip Applied:_____Date: _____
Tip Mastered: _____Date: _____

December 8

Laughter

It was my husband's idea one year to go to a tree farm and cut down our very own tree! That was a big mistake I decided!

The ground was covered with heavy snow, and the few vehicles parked along the road were far from us. Our vehicle became stuck in the snow, and we could not push it out. In the back seat, our two granddaughters were crying. At last, someone drove by. After stepping out of the vehicle, I held my arms up and yelled for help! Two men started pushing us out of the hole. After that experience, we never chopped another tree down again!

December 9

Charity

Don't miss taking pictures of your family, parties, and gift-giving.

Homework

Share them on social media, especially for those who are out-of-state, so everyone can enjoy them. Spread the joy!

Assignment:

Tip Applied:_____Date: _____
Tip Mastered: _____Date: _____

December 10

Time Management

Many stores and restaurants provide curbside pickups and deliveries.

Homework

If you want the store to shop for you, there is a fee, but it is worth it. You can simply put your purchases away once they are delivered. Whether placing your order over the phone or computer, it doesn't take long.

Assignment:

Tip Applied:_____Date: _____
Tip Mastered: _____Date: _____

December 11

Time Management

Cut down the prep time for cleaning, chopping, or shredding vegetables and fruits.

Homework

Purchase healthy foods in ready-to-eat portions. It is a little more expensive, but it will save time during the holidays.

Assignment:

Tip Applied:_____Date: _____

Tip Mastered: _____Date: _____

December 12

Laughter

Each year my husband insists we buy a live tree, but I prefer a pre-lit artificial tree. (I still remember getting stuck in the snow at the tree farm.)

Putting up a live tree can be a hassle, especially when placing it in a stand. We would spend an hour saying "Move to the left," "Now move it to the right," "It is crooked again!" and we had to start all over. I got to the point where I was ready to throw it to the curb! So, we took the plunge the following year, and purchased a pre-lit artificial tree that was easy to put up. No more hassles!

December 13

Spirituality & Time Management

"Then the kingdom of heaven will be comparable to ten virgins, who took their lamps and went out to meet the groom. Five of them were foolish, and were prudent. For when the foolish took their lamps, they did not take extra oil with them; but the prudent ones took oil in flasks with their lamps" (Matthew 25:1-4, NASB).

There were ten virgins waiting for the bridegroom to show up without any notice. Only five virgins had extra oil and the other five did not. When they left to purchase extra oil at the store, the bridegroom appeared, and the five wise virgins entered the wedding feast together with him, closing the door. Notice how the virgins who had extra oil were well-organized? They clearly demonstrated time management.

December 14

Tip

Find any ornaments that are cracked, peeling, or just plain old?

Homework

You could repurpose them into a wreath, floral arrangement, or paint the ornaments. Give one to someone as a gift. See many ideas on Pinterest.

Assignment:

Tip Applied:_____Date: _____
Tip Mastered: _____Date: _____

December 15

Organization & Time Management

What is the best way to organize all the gifts around the tree for each person?

Homework

In the dollar store, you can find the largest dollar bags. Fill them all with gifts for the same person in the large bag. Gifts should be wrapped or in smaller gift bags with tissue paper inside a large bag. This way all the gifts for that person are in the bag and won't be forgotten.

Assignment:

Tip Applied:_____Date: _____
Tip Mastered: _____Date: _____

December 16

Time Management

Are you working and don't have time to shop and run errands?

Homework

Eat lunch at your desk, and then run an errand or pick up a few things during lunch. This will save time when on your way home.

Assignment:

Tip Applied:_____Date: _____
Tip Mastered: _____Date: _____

December 17

Time Management

If you are hosting a Christmas dinner or get-together, sharing responsibility for cooking the meal can make things easier.

Homework

Invite family and friends to bring a side dish, appetizer, or dessert. Your life will be easier if everyone contributes. Invite guests and list the menu items so they can choose one or two items to avoid duplication.

To help with event planning, you can Google a number of applications such as Facebook, Party Swizzle, Evite, Smilebox, and so forth. The applications come with checklists, themes, invitations, menus, RSVPs, and more.

Assignment:

Tip Applied:_____Date: _____
Tip Mastered: _____Date: _____

December 18

Etiquette

Are you going to a party, fellowship, or get-together?

Homework

A good rule is to never arrive at someone's home empty-handed. Bring a thoughtful gift they can use after the party. The gift can be anything from a bottle of wine, an ornament, or a box of chocolates to homemade baked goods, specialty teas, coffee, flowers, and so forth.

Assignment:

Tip Applied:_____Date: _____
Tip Mastered: _____Date: _____

December 19

Laughter

"After the Christmas pageant, I asked my six-year-old son if he remembered the gifts that the wise men brought Jesus. He thought for a minute, then said: 'Gold, Frankenstein, and humor.'"

Actual children's versions of Christmas Carols:

- " . . . sleep in heavenly peas"
- "Joy to the world, the Savior rains"
- "This is he whom Sears of old"
- "Angels we have heard on high, sweetly singing o'er the plane"
- "While shepherds washed their socks by night"

Source:
https://javacasa.com/humor/seasonal.htm

December 20

Spirituality

"And He said to them, 'Come away by yourselves to a secluded place and rest a little while.' (For there were many people coming and going, and they did not even have time to eat)" (Mark 6:31, NASB).

Homework

The holiday season should not be all work and no play. You can have fun with your family and friends while playing games, watching movies, engaging in Christmas activities, ice-skating, and building a snowman. Put yourself out there and make memories!

Assignment:

Tip Applied:_____Date: _____
Tip Mastered: _____Date: _____

December 21

Organization & Time Management

You probably think it's silly but find someone to be responsible for putting the wrapping paper in a trash bag when opening gifts.

Homework

Play a game and toss the wrapping paper into the trash bag. Save the gift bags and put the tissue paper in the bag and / or fireplace. Cleanup will be a breeze.

Assignment:

Tip Applied:_____Date: _____
Tip Mastered: _____Date: _____

December 22

Time Management

Do you have vacation time coming up?

Homework

If so, spend some time catching up on all the holiday activities, parties, and chores. Also, it is a great time to organize a room, closet, office, or area that has been neglected and bothering you. After that, rest your body.

Assignment:

Tip Applied:_____Date: _____
Tip Mastered: _____Date: _____

December 23

Time Management

There are two days left before Christmas! What should you do first?

Homework

Finish your last-minute shopping. Make time to wrap gifts, cook, and / or buy a meal for attending a family gathering. Prioritize your tasks so that you do not feel rushed.

Assignment:

Tip Applied:_____Date: _____
Tip Mastered: _____Date: _____

December 24

Etiquette

Teach your children to say, "Thank you!"

Homework

When they have finished opening their gifts, ask them to go around the room and say, "Thank you" and give each person a hug. Adults should do the same. By teaching them proper etiquette and manners when they are small, they will carry it into adulthood.

I remember on our way to a relative's house, my mom would say, "Give your aunt a kiss and a hug when we get there." I asked, "Do we have to?" The hug and kiss blessed them. I continued the tradition, and it has become a blessed habit. It may take years if they have never done it before, but they will return it someday.

Assignment:

Tip Applied:_____Date: _____
Tip Mastered: _____Date: _____

December 25

Spirituality

Christmas Day!

"Where is He who has been born king of the Jews? For we saw His star when it rose and have come to worship Him" (Matthew 2:2, ESV).

Homework

Take advantage of this time to spend with your family and to give thanks for all your blessings! Open one gift at a time, with each person taking their turn around the room. Everybody can see the gift they received and from whom it came. Jesus is to be praised for the gifts. Happy birthday Jesus!

Assignment:

Tip Applied:_____Date: _____
Tip Mastered: _____Date: _____

December 26

Organization

Christmas storage bins are available for almost everything.

Homework

Containers and storage solutions can be found for wreaths, artificial trees, ribbons, wrapping paper, ornaments, lights, Christmas cards, and so forth. Most of these items go down in price after Christmas. Go shopping and get organized!

Assignment:

Tip Applied:_____Date: _____
Tip Mastered: _____Date: _____

December 27

Laughter

Two young boys were spending the night at their grandparents' house the week before Christmas. At bedtime, the two boys knelt beside their beds to say their prayers. The younger one began praying at the top of his lungs:

"I pray for a new bicycle."
"I pray for a new Xbox."
His older brother leaned over, nudged him, and said, "Why are you shouting? God isn't deaf." To which the little brother replied, "No, but Grandma is!"

Source:
https://www.javacasa.com/humor/seasonal.htm

Q. What do donkeys send out near Christmas?
A. Mule-tide greetings.

Q. What did Adam say the day before Christmas?
A. It's Christmas Eve!

Source:
https://christiancamppro.com/the-constantly-growing-list-of-funny-christian-jokes-with-pictures/

 # December 28

Spirituality & Charity

"But Zaccheus stopped and said to the Lord, 'Behold, Lord, half of my possessions I am giving to the poor, and if I have extorted anything from anyone, I am giving back four times as much'" (Luke 19:8, NASB).

Homework

You still have three days left to give to a charity before the end of the year to receive a tax break. A donation center is also a great place to donate clothing and / or household items. You can give to a ministry, church, and / or online charity. Thank you for your generous contribution!

Assignment:

Tip Applied:_____Date: _____
Tip Mastered: _____Date: _____

December 29

Organization

Taking down the tree is easier and faster than putting it up. Are you a person who would like to take it down before New Year's Day?

Homework

Donate the ornaments you no longer need or want. If your ornaments are expensive, wrap and put them in an ornament plastic container. Use the containers you just bought and pack all decorations in plastic storage containers and store them away. It is a great feeling when everything is organized and put away until next year.

Assignment:

Tip Applied:_____Date: _____
Tip Mastered: _____Date: _____

December 30

Spirituality

"Come to Me, all who are weary and burdened, and I will give you rest" (Matthew 11:28, NASB).

Homework

Get some rest! Let your body rest by sleeping in, taking a nap, watching movies, and relaxing to refresh your body. Recreation and relaxation are self-explanatory categories; they are times to enjoy when all other responsibilities are fulfilled.

Assignment:

Tip Applied:_____Date: _____
Tip Mastered: _____Date: _____

December 31

Tip

Ringing in the New Year by attending parties, along with holiday fatigue, is exhausting.

Homework

Instead, have a nice quiet dinner and movie if you decide not to go to the party. Embrace the New Year with positivity, resolutions, and happy goals. Take full advantage of the organizational skills offered in this calendar. What number of tips did you manage to accomplish? Let's begin again on January 1st and see how many more tips you can achieve over the next twelve months!

Assignment:

Tip Applied:_____Date: _____
Tip Mastered: _____Date: _____

List of Abbreviations

Home:
In professional organizing, this universal word refers to a physical location where an item resides. Restoring an item to its home requires taking it out of its home and placing it back. In this way, it is always organized, and you can find it immediately.

Clutter:
When your living space is cluttered, so is your mind and you can't think! Everything must have a designated home. It takes discipline to keep it up and return things to their place.

Homework:
Most of my clients receive homework after we're done with an organizing session. In addition to saving them time, it also saves them money. They are delighted with the results when they do their homework, and I am as well.

Those who realize they can make a profit from selling unused items may be more willing to relinquish an item. You can make extra money by selling your items at consignment stores.

Sort:
To put in a certain place or rank according to kind, class, or nature.

Source:
Specify the source of something, such as quoted material, a firsthand document, or primary reference work.

Additional Words Professional Organizers Use:

The Bin Theory:
Start with bins, plastic bags and / or baskets, each with one of the following labels: KEEP, DONATE, PURGE, SHRED, RECYCLE and CONSIGNMENT. Begin with a room and pick up one item at a time and put it in the proper bin. Keep going until the room is free of clutter. Take the appropriate action with each bin as to where to redistribute the contents.

Solutions:
Solutions are available to end the clutter in homes today and into the future. Why live with the stress of having to dig through clutter to find that needed item? Organizing will help you find any object in seconds and keep the clutter from returning.

Piles of Clutter:
Homeowners sometimes have piles of clutter everywhere, on tabletop surfaces, on floors, and even on beds and sofas. Some are perfectionists who will not be satisfied unless everything is perfect. Many clients are overwhelmed with stuff and are unsure of "where" to start, let alone "how" to proceed.

Problems:
- ✓ Closets too cramped to fit in clothes
- ✓ Piles of unopened, unsorted mail
- ✓ Childrens' rooms are a disaster
- ✓ Can't see the floor in a teenager's room
- ✓ Dysfunctional home office

- ✓ The filing system is so old and crowded, current papers can't be filed
- ✓ Takes too long to find a document
- ✓ Apartment or condo storage unit has not been touched in years
- ✓ Death of a parent requires distribution of household goods and / or organization for an estate sale
- ✓ Embarrassed to have people over due to clutter

Methods:

The key to organizing is learning a method and staying disciplined. The process begins with time management. Schedules need to be arranged to fit in various chores before leaving the house, when coming home, and before going to bed. So many people are busy, but once they are organized, they can learn to stay that way.

Medical Terminology:

I worked with many clients with ADHD: Attention-deficit/hyperactivity disorder. OCD: Obsessive Compulsive Disorder, CD: Chronic Disorganization and Hoarding.

NAPO:

The National Association of Productivity & Organizing Professionals is recognized as the association for professional organizers. NAPO offers organizers opportunities to sharpen their skills through on-going education and professional development. NAPO has a Code of Ethics by which members are expected to abide. A professional organizer who is a NAPO member has made a commitment to his/her business and to our clients.

Biblical:

One scripture is copied exactly from the Bible including the version and reference.

Sinner's Prayer:
Many of the scriptures in this book are about asking Jesus into your heart. Once you receive Jesus into your heart, the Holy Spirit comes in and takes over.

Pray this prayer:
Lord Jesus, this is my simple prayer to you. I know that I am a sinner and that I often fall short of the glory of God. No longer will I close the door when I hear You knocking. By faith, I gratefully receive Your gift of salvation. I'm ready to trust You as my Lord and Savior. Thank You, Lord Jesus, for coming to Earth. I believe You are the Son of God who died on the cross for my sins and rose from the dead on the third day. Thank You for Your forgiveness of sins and for giving me the gift of eternal life. I invite Jesus to come into my heart and be my Savior. In the name of Jesus, Amen.

It is important to faithfully attend a church with born-again believers. You need to grow in the Bible and your life will be changed. You don't need to force it, but it will come. Be patient with yourself and give Jesus a chance. He loves you with unconditional love no matter what you have done!

About the Author

Deborah Rae Tebbe founded Organized Happy Helper, LLC in 2004. She continues to manage the business still today.

This book is her passion for helping many people become organized with the idea of accountability by giving her readers a daily homework assignment.

In addition to earning many certificates, conducting presentations, and organizing residential and commercial projects, she has been featured in several newspaper articles. Debbie has coordinated and organized over a thousand clients.

To make sure they could learn these tips on their own, she always gave them homework. Her goal has been to help clients save time and money.

https://www.organizedhappyhelper.com
Email: organizedhh@gmail.com

Achieved Certificates:

- NAPO Specialist, Residential Organizing Certificate (2017)
- NAPO Specialist, Workplace Productivity Certificate (2017)
- NAPO Specialist, Household Management Certificate (2020)
- NAPO Golden Circle 15 Years (2019)
- ICD Institute for Challenging Disorganization is the current name from: National Study Group of Chronic Disorganization (NSGCD), CD-Specialist, Level II (2007)

Achievements:

- Moves for Seniors; previously as a (Premier Senior Move Facilitator).
- Attended seven NAPO conferences around the United States.
- Held five Board of Director positions for the NAPO Michigan Chapter.
- Before organizing, I worked in the corporate field with administrative skills and as an IT computer specialist.
- **Residential Services**: Consultation, Clutter Solutions, Storage Solutions, Interior Design, Floral Design, Garage Sales, Errands and Shopping, Planning for Loved Ones, Public Speaking, Packing for Moves, and Selling on eBay.
- **Business Services**: Office Efficiency, Work Space, Work Environment, Computer Assistance, Training Sessions, Public Speaking, Time Management, Set-up filing systems, Work Efficiency, Streamline the Workflow, Work Space Clutter, etc.
- **Volunteer Work:** NAPO Michigan members for Habitat for Humanity, Gleaners Food Donation Center, Jewish Center for Mentally Challenged and Homeless Shelter in Ypsilanti, Michigan. Imago Dei Crisis Pregnancy Center for fifteen years as an organizer and teaching filing to pregnant and new mothers.
- **Newspaper Articles:** St. Clair Shores Sentinel, Macomb Daily, The Detroit News, Michigan Lawyers Weekly 2006, and The Manchester Enterprise (Ypsilanti)
- Additionally, featured articles in organizing websites.

Printed in the United States
by Baker & Taylor Publisher Services